YOUR TICKET TO SUCCESS

To two incredible mothers for support beyond belief:

Sylvia McMillan
Vi Woods

YOUR TICKET TO SUCCESS

the definitive guide to
NLP in selling

Alex McMillan

2000

First published in Great Britain in 1997 by Management Books 2000 Ltd, Cowcombe House, Cowcombe Hill, Chalford, Gloucestershire GL6 8HP Tel: 01285-760722. Fax: 01285-760708

Printed and bound in Great Britain by The Orbital Press, Letchworth

British Library Cataloguing in Publication Data is available

ISBN 1-85252-281-X

Acknowledgements

I would like to thank the many friends, loved ones. supporters, delegates on courses, business partners, employees, other authors and clients who have supported me in various ways in producing this work to help as many people as possible in their business careers.

I would like to thank my mother for her tremendous support and belief, and for being a model of excellence in communication – particularly in the art of developing a deep and near instant rapport with everyone she meets.

Other models of specific excellence that I have studied and learnt from include: my father, Alex McMillan (Senior) for being one of the few people that have truly mastered the art of clear and lucid communication; Richard Lowden for maintaining enthusiasm, determination and motivation, no matter what; Gary Thompson for excellence in listening and negotiation skills.

My thanks also to Douglas Woods for much moral support, to Neil Carson and Tracy McMillan for proof reading, and to Tracy, Alex, Zoe and Naomi for family love and support.

Preface

This book is essential reading for anybody in the following categories:

- Sales and other customer service professionals
- Non-sales professionals wishing to improve their persuasion skills
- Negotiators
- Personnel professionals
- People seeking a better paid job
- Presenters and trainers
- Anyone who believes they would benefit by transforming their influencing power.

This book is a gold mine, full of simple tips learnt by studying and modelling top sales professionals. The techniques can be applied by every business professional who is serious about making more money for him/herself and their employing organisation. The techniques are tried, tested and work with profound results. Your performance will improve substantially whatever it is that you do and at whatever level. (As an alternative try learning by your own mistakes and experience over the next ten years!).

During my career I have read many books on sales and attended many courses. The emphasis has always been on 'professional selling', which means looking after the customer's needs. To me the words that they use – 'Prospect', 'Cold Call', 'Pitching', 'Closing', 'Objection Handling', 'Sales Representative', 'Win Win negotiation' – do not suggest that the customer or potential customer's needs are being put first. 'Win Win', while sounding very ethical, suggests to me that there is an Us/Them contest going on. The belief that selling is a contest has dominated sales training for years, there has been no new thinking or approaches. When somebody gives you a business card that says 'Sales Representative', what does that imply? To me it implies that their only objective is to procure sales for their company and earn commission. Nothing wrong with that, but when I buy from somebody I choose people that convince me that they serve me. Try a business card that says 'Customer Service Representative', AND LIVE UP TO IT – believe me, you will have a lot more happy customers that remember you. Next time you are being 'sold' to, think how much it excites and motivates you that you are a prospect that has been cold called and closed on!

Most customers have become very weary and resistant to traditional mechanistic selling methods. A new age is upon us for those who wish to be true sales professionals. The emphasis I suggest for this new age is on rapport, trust, listening.... (When was the last time you experienced a sales representative use that one?) Every hour of every day more than £10 billion changes hands in London alone. People like spending money – that is why they work so hard for it. Selling is not difficult. All you need to do is apply half of the principles in this book and you will outperform hard-boiled sales professionals with years of experience behind them. Yes, really, I have proved just that many times.

The emphasis of traditional selling has been on 'closing'. My belief (based on what I found by studying top sales professionals instead of designing theories) is that the emphasis has to be on 'opening' sales opportunities. To me the term closing suggests a door which is being shut to lock the customer into the deal. For business in the 90's we need to think in terms of finding 'keys' to let future customers in. I know that most future potential customers want to be present customers and what we are doing or saying is somehow stopping them, putting them off. The challenge of professional selling is finding out (searching for the key to the door) what you can say or do differently to let them in as customers.

This book covers the latest developments in communication techniques, which have been substantial in recent years. It deals with techniques that have been developed particularly from NLP (Neuro Linguistic Programming), and my own behavioural modelling of various top persuaders. Chapter 1 explains the concept of NLP, and how it can be used to transform your business performance. Chapters 2 to 10 examine the specific techniques in detail.

In short, read and apply the principles in this book and you will increase the quality and quantity of your business performance to a level to which neither your peers nor even you yourself at this point dare aspire. This is my personal guarantee to you. There are too many sales professionals out there who read books and 'know what to do'. Doing what you know is the key – apply your learnings, adapt them, get experience of them....

Alex McMillan
January 1997

Contents

Contents

1

Introduction

A. Success Express

'Success Express' is an advanced selling system, not only for sales people but anyone who wants a real edge – even the novice who wants to beat the professional. It is advanced in terms of techniques and results, in contrast to traditional selling. It does not require previous knowledge, lengthy study or experience. It does, however, require practice in the various techniques. Practice provides you with your own feedback and thus refinement of the effect of these techniques. This in turn will change your perception as to what you can achieve. Then you will develop habits, automatic competence in applying the techniques. After applying the ideas in the following chapters, you will start to appreciate that you do not need to be born with the gift of the gab in order to excel in your communications with others.

The ideas in this book utilise and develop knowledge from a diverse cross section of academic and practical disciplines. Neuro Linguistic Programming (NLP), the new psychology of achievement, has contributed a great deal. However most of the material presently available on this subject is in a raw form, full of academic jargon, and needs to be interpreted in order to be of practical use in business. I have also avoided 'explanations of why' and concentrate on the practical usage of techniques. If you are the sort of person who likes to boast how many closing techniques you know or to show off the latest buzzwords then look elsewhere. If, on the other hand, you want to transform your communication and influencing skills, magnifying your results, read on.

I believe that the selling techniques of pre-recession days, with the emphasis on closing, are not enough to get ahead in today's business environment. Buyers have evolved, hardened and become very sophisticated. We need to become professional in our approach. The word 'professional' has previously been bandied about meaning the application of the same mechanistic closing techniques in every situation. We need to respond to varied communication and thinking patterns. The Success Express is a communication system that responds to this need for more professionalism. Those who not only learn it, but apply it, will accelerate their own and their company's success. If you learn, apply, practise and master the ideas that follow you will find that your ability to develop rapport, listen, understand, be flexible and influence will be better than you currently believe possible. This belief change in itself will empower you to greater performance. Suspend scepticism, try it out and see the results. Dismiss this challenge and you will come second to those that take it!

People are happy to be influenced if it improves their situation. Before we can really master the influencing of others it is important to understand how we are influenced by others ourselves, in situations that improve or limit our lives. Where have all your influences come from? How did you form your opinions, values and beliefs about anything? How are these opinions, values and beliefs different from those of other people you know? How did they come to be influenced differently? When you are influenced you are usually accepting the lead from somebody else because they gained a rapport with you – they have communicated or explained their position to you in a way you can understand and appreciate.

When running training sessions one rather straightforward (or is it?) exercise I often finish with is as follows. 'In groups over the next ten minutes decide on a meal out that you will all go to following the course.' Then I stand back and observe. Immediately, all group members are clearly influencing each other, in a variety of ways, even if they remain silent. Are they going to elect a leader? If so, who will pitch for it and who will manoeuvre to avoid it? Who is being led? Who has set clear objectives? When you have observed a straightforward decision like this and observed the patterns of influence you start to appreciate more and more why coming to complex and important business decisions is a more complicated process than it first appears. Selling your ideas to others requires mastery at communication. NLP is mastery of communication. This book shows you through the maze with tremendous short cuts, avoiding the need to learn by long and painful experience – which can itself lead to the wrong or limiting conclusions.

Influencing forces are at work all the time which cannot be stopped. The important thing is to take control and harness these forces to ensure clear rapport and thus communication leading to well defined outcomes. Have you ever been in a situation where you have communicated something with good intent to somebody and they have reacted negatively, despite your (to you) good intention? Perhaps finished by saying, "What did I say?" After studying this book you will be able accurately to predict the response to your communications, taking control of your desired outcomes.

To the person who is reading on to take that challenge, welcome to what you will look back on as being the first day of the transformation of your career.

Let us now look at some basic principles of psychology that set a foundation for the chapters that follow. All human memory is a distortion of experience, an internal representation of an event. Our conscious mind finds repetition boring, yet our unconscious mind, which makes most purchase decisions, thrives on it. Look at the success of McDonalds – limited menu choice, same seating and layout of restaurants throughout the world.

We all perceive a situation differently. If there is a car crash outside your office now with ten eye witnesses the chances are the police and insurance authorities will get ten different versions of what happened. Each will be totally convinced theirs is the only version. Why is this? Well we filter reality through what basically boils down to three distinct processes: generalisation, deletion and distortion. Our brain does this automatically. It generalises and deletes to cut down the sheer volume of information coming to us. Perceptions of events are like fingerprints, different for everyone. Can you describe to me the details of all the cars you passed on your way to work this morning. At any instant of the journey can you describe in detail all the sights and sounds of everything going on around you. No, in fact we filter out more than 99% of the detail around us to stop our brains being overwhelmed by concentrating on what has meaning for us. Distortion is the interesting one. What happens here, is that we compare new information and experience unconsciously to all our previous experiences. These previous experiences will have created habits, opinions, values and beliefs. We then distort the new information to fit into our reference frame. This is how we make meaning of new events. Let us have a look at the three processes in a practical example.

Steve, a friend of mine, recently went to New York. He got out of the airport and hailed a cab. When he got out the driver swore at him for not leaving a tip. When he got to his meeting he retold his story. His colleagues said that their cab rides had been fine. On returning to the UK, Jonathan a friend of his was due to leave for New York and asked for any pointers.

'What ever you do, don't travel by cab. The cab drivers are rude (generalisation), and they drive recklessly (distortion). 'He did not mention that all his colleagues had no problems with the cab drivers (deletion). What is worse Harry now has this story in his (unconscious) mind as a reference piece of information.

Do you see how important all this is for commercial communication. Everything anybody (a customer) has been previously told will have been 'filtered' in this way. The total picture it makes up will be reality for him. Saying any different will just conflict with what he knows to be true for his 'model of how the world goes around'. So the first essential thing to be aware of is that you are selling to his reality, not yours or anybody else's. The second important thing is to be able to reach that prospect in your communication. The chapters that follow show you how to talk to someone with total respect for their 'model of the world' without the need of substantial knowledge of that person. It is in fact easier to achieve than you might imagine with

NLP, the new technology of achievement, and the results you get will surprise you. You do not need any information other than what they give you in conversation. This book in essence is all about how we can reach the recipient of your communication in his world. That to me is the difference between professional communication and learning techniques by repeating 'parrot fashion'.

Remember that customers – prospects/interviewers, interviewees, staff, superiors – believe that their model of the world is the real world. And for them they will always be right. 'Reality leaves a lot to the imagination!'

Many people I have talked to have asked me about NLP and NLP business skills training. Before we proceed I have included a brief background that you will find useful.

B. Background To Neuro Linguistic Programming (NLP)

In the early 1970's at the University Of California two men came together: Richard Bandler, a computer scientist, gestalt therapist and mathematician, and John Grinder, the Professor Of Linguistics. Their plan was to model people who were making significant changes in others' behaviour. They initially studied three world class therapists: Fritz Perls, Virginia Satir and Milton Erickson. These therapists were at the top of their professions, creating dramatic and quick, yet long-term change in their clients. From these extensive studies Bandler and Grinder produced a blueprint for peak performance. This model they called Neuro Linguistic Programming (NLP).

NLP is essentially a model of excellence and achievement – 'what works best'. It offers a systematic way of consistently achieving out-standing results across a broad spectrum of communication.

NLP is the answer to the question, 'What is it that makes the difference between somebody who is merely competent at any given skill, and somebody who excels at the same skill?' This question has led to a whole new understanding that has revolutionised the field of psychology, and hence selling – how we perceive the world and how we organise our thinking, feeling, skills and behaviour. NLP is still evolving, and is the subject of continuing innovation, development and exploding worldwide interest. It can be used remedially, so that, for example, if someone is not getting what they want out of life, it can enable them to uncover, change or transform what is holding them back. It can also be used generatively to enable them to make enhancements – i.e. to achieve excellence in something they already perform well, often when they believed they had already reached the limit of their ability.

NLP involves the gathering of information to make models, based on the internal, often unconscious, experiences of the subjects. Try asking a top sales person why they are so good. They don't know – they just are. Their techniques, patterns, beliefs, skills, values are all things that they live and do instinctively.

NEURO...   An understanding of the brain and it's func-tions. The nervous system through which experience is received and processed through the five senses.

LINGUISTIC...   Verbal and Non-Verbal Communication to ourselves and others. Language and non verbal communication systems through which neural representations are coded, ordered, and given meaning.

PROGRAMMING   Behaviour and thinking patterns. The ability to organize our communication and neuro-logical systems to achieve specific desired goals and results.

NLP is the study of the structure of subjective experience. As such it is not about theories, which is the basis of most other psychologies and science generally. Looking at human nature from this different standpoint was the key ingredient to what has led to such a treasure chest of discoveries.

Bandler and Grinder developed a unique system of asking questions to gather precise information. The more they studied top performers the more they noticed about how we communicate – and the more they noticed the differences between the average and the outstanding.

They successfully transferred these communication patterns to others (without extensive training) and they too produced outstanding results. Clearly an unprecedented quantum leap had been made in accelerating the learning process. From the early work, research and development has been continued. Documentation on the successes of the application of NLP is hard to believe, though there is now substantial evidence. For years now Dr Bandler has studied how geniuses used their minds to accomplish what they did and has repeatedly replicated the results that they got – so successfully that NLP is now a well established international phenomenon.

NLP Modelling is the process of replicating particular behaviours. To model effectively certain skills are required which include sensory awareness, verbal and non-verbal skills to elicit quality information. There are three key areas of behaviour to model: belief systems, strategies and physiology. The test for the model is in producing the same, or similar results in someone else. An important distinction is to be made between theories and models. A theory is more concerned with answering 'Why' questions. A model is concerned with answering 'How?'. Modelling is the process that requires knowing 'What to do' to answer 'How?'.

The first step of NLP modelling is to find a skill that you would like to have. The second stage is to find somebody who excels at that skill. Then the NLP Practitioner studies that person until they have established how exactly they do that. This is then tested on others until clearly the patterns that make the difference have been identified. This modelling process is quite complex and developing in sophistication all the time. There are now other disciplines and research being carried out taking these ideas further. It is not however necessary to understand or even appreciate the modelling process to benefit from NLP. In fact all that is necessary is to adopt the patterns of behaviour of outstanding performers found from somebody else's modelling of them. Rapport and motivation skills, for example, have been studied so much by NLP experts that there is a great wealth of knowledge available. This book is not about the modelling process itself; it is the result of behavioural modelling of sales superstars. (Please be aware that most courses on NLP will be about learning the trail of techniques that have been left by NLP modellers not the modelling process itself.)

It has long been known that we communicate in three ways: through the words we use, tonality and body language. What is less widely known is the influence of each category. One often quoted major study concluded that they are Words 7%, Tonality 38% and Body Language 55%. (Please note that to draw accurate conclusions from any study the parameters and objectives of what was being measured have to be looked at. Secondly this short conclusion ignores the substantial overlap between the three; they are clearly not separate. Even so, the implications for business communication are far reaching.) In business if your sales force are trained only in what to say they are missing out on 93% of their potential! NLP teaches how to develop rapport in seconds by using 100% of communication channels. In the area of words, sales scripts, questions, closing techniques and above all listening skills have been revolutionised. The advanced language patterns of NLP can teach excellence in communication skills. NLP, then, is the art and science of achievement. It has only recently arrived in the UK business community, although well established in the medical and educational professions.

NLP is the study of the difference between competence and excellence, in terms of practical skills that can be passed on to others. It is therefore a learning model. In addition to modelling and the resultant methodology there are also the NLP presuppositions. These are the model of the attitudes and beliefs that have been found to be true for the top communicators and in people who are very successful at what they do.

C. NLP Business Training

In the USA the business community started to take an interest. Extensive research was carried out from Fortune 500 companies on their highest performing sales staff. Dramatic and quick results were achieved and are well documented. Rumours about the wonders of Neuro Linguistic Programming in business abound. NLP does work; it will bring a new level of creativity and performance to any company's sales. NLP technology enables us to teach high performance to a level never previously available in management training.

Most sales and management training and philosophies are useful for gaining intellectual knowledge about achieving excellence, or getting us excited or motivated. Most do not teach us skills that result in changing our daily behaviour. NLP offers the ways for us to make the changes for the results we want by building on the resources we already possess.

The decision to take NLP-based business training is an important one; it is also a difficult one. People are by nature more comfortable with something that they are familiar with – something tried and tested from somebody that understands their industry's needs and issues. To get a real edge in business, I believe that you have to do something different from your competitors. After all, if you do all the things they do, surely the best you can achieve is the same as them. Those who want to be their industry's leaders have to step bravely forward and take the calculated chances. The only real reference to the value of a training programme is the actual improvements it has given to your staff over time. Short-term hype and motivation for a couple of weeks won't usually pay for the lost sales time in attending courses – and what has been achieved for another company may be a good indicator but it does not necessarily mean that you will gain the same benefits.

Can you study books or videos on NLP to learn the new ideas? Well, yes, but you have to remember that selling is a behavioural practical skill. Try learning to swim or drive a car from a book or video.

Let me briefly explain about learning.

We each have a conscious and unconscious mind, typically, though not always left (conscious) and right (unconscious). The conscious mind deals with everything that is in your awareness at any given time. The unconscious is everything else – i.e. all your memories and programmes (habits). When you get on the phone or make a presentation you will be running unconscious programmes that have been set up to achieve the results you want. In short we call this experience.

Now with NLP we have modelled the programmes or patterns of behaviour of peak performers in various fields. Those patterns will be analysed logically and considered by your conscious mind. The conscious mind will challenge the new ideas with disbelief and scepticism while referring to unconscious 'files' of previous experiences that either support or challenge this.

Now, knowing the best ways to produce your desired results is only half the battle: the next step is to attain 'unconscious competence' or habits in those skills. After training you do not have to rely on thinking about applying what you have learnt. Students apply new habits automatically without necessarily being aware that they have changed. The big limitation to training is that clearly and professionally communicated good ideas are often forgotten a week later. The learning might only get as far as your conscious mind (current awareness). Now your conscious mind can only process a maximum of nine 'chunks' of information at a time. If you attend a day course with forty new ideas in it and make a sales presentation the next day imagine what will happen.

First, you will use up at least six chunks of conscious awareness just listening and observing your client and thinking of what to say next. That does not leave you a lot of processing ability to apply the new sales skills you have learned. NLP training tells you how the world's best produce that result, then develops the habit in you. Many courses teach you what to do, but few teach you how to do it in the precise way made possible by NLP.

Think about your sales department. Who is consistently the top performer? How do they do that? Ask them, ask their peers, ask their customers. You are unlikely to find the real or full answer. If you can, why have you not got everybody emulating them to the same level of performance? NLP modellers have extensively modelled top sales people, looking for the difference that makes the difference. They could have taken ten years of experience to develop those patterns of behaviour. You can learn them in days. This is hard to believe but research has established that the brain does not take a long time to change. On the contrary, change is naturally fast.

In traditional sales training, delegates are taught that they have to agree with the prospect. I have seen reminders such as 'Agree And Outweigh' or 'Win Arguments, Lose Sales' on the walls of several sales offices. This is because disagreement is believed to break rapport. What they fail to recognise is that rapport can be made, maintained and enhanced at many more levels than mere content. Therefore NLP-based selling has no requirement for the 'bull' and 'lying' that the traditional approach can so easily lead to, giving sales professionals a bad reputation. NLP can provide you with all sorts of amazing techniques for establishing rapport. The first step is rapport with yourself, which in NLP is referred to as 'congruence'. If you send out conflicting messages you will lose respect and credibility. People who are out of harmony or rapport with themselves are hardly likely to develop harmony in their relationships with others. That is when they revert to bullying, lying or other forms of coercion to win through.

Ironically, the benefits of NLP sales and business communication training are so great they are the major obstacle to selling NLP-based training courses. The obstacle is at the level of belief.

Investing in NLP training is different, exciting, fun to learn, and it works. It enables us to create more of the results that we want by making us more effective, faster. With these skills, modelled from unusually talented people, you can transform your performance. Your results will be dramatically improved.

If possible see them in action. Take up references. Be careful of differentiating between delegates who enjoyed a course and those that increased their performance following it. Whether or not people speak well of a training programme is not necessarily an indication of success. Know your objectives for the programme and measure success against these criteria. Look for proven expertise and track record.

But be careful – someone who has bought into and been trained in old methods has got an interest in avoiding progression of new ideas. What NLP qualifications do the trainers have? Are they recognised? If so by whom? Bear in mind that the only Institute that Richard Bandler, the creator of NLP, recognises is The Society Of NLP, which is developing material by the week. Techniques of one year ago have been surpassed. Are they keeping up to date? What original research and development is being carried out? Are they just rehashing somebody else's ideas? NLP is enjoying an enormous upsurge in interest and many trainers are getting on the bandwagon before they have really mastered the skills themselves. So be very careful.

Some training programmes merely present ideas. Avoid these, it is much cheaper to buy some books, just to get ideas. Look for development of delegate confidence and competence in carrying out new skills. Training people is a very professional skill. Having a dynamic presentation is not enough. You can go to a rock concert to be entertained (if you like rock music); it doesn't mean that you have learnt anything. Ask the training company what techniques they use in their programme. Tell them what your objectives are and ask what they would do to achieve them.

D. Are NLP Techniques Manipulative?

Yes. I wish to give readers the abilities to listen, understand and communicate back effectively and in so doing dovetail outcomes – in other words, to manipulate the client's and your resources in order to leave you both better off than before. If that dovetailing of outcomes is not present at the end, then the deal should not have gone ahead. Pushing somebody into something that they later regret is manipulating them for your benefit only and is clearly unethical unprofessional behaviour. In practice this style of sales person tends to defeat himself. They don't get referrals, recommendations or repeat business. For long-term sales success these are essential ingredients.

Most people buy on emotion and then rationalise and fit logic to their decision. They even believe that they made the decision based on logic. If we really made 'logical' purchasing decisions, who would buy cigarettes, expensive French after-shaves, junk food, scratch cards, gold cards, etc.? This means that professional sales people have got to consider ethics. It also explains so many frustrated sales people who met the customer's needs with matching benefits and wonder why they still did not get the order.

Sales people have needs too. They need to hit target to keep their job. They have other potential customers to talk to. They have a mortgage to pay. The real top performers are the ones who are neither 'nice guy' nor ruthless, but the ones who can dovetail their own and their company's needs with the needs of a future client. You will soon come to appreciate in this book that top persuaders don't have some secret strategy or formula; they are totally flexible and respond to their future clients' patterns of communicating.

Practising and developing NLP skills can be compared to learning how to swim. With a book alone, could reading the book – even repeatedly – develop you into a great swimmer? Certainly not. The point is practice. Experiment and explore with the ideas in this book. That is the way you will change from knowing of a technique to mastery of it.

I have taken great steps to avoid jargon, other technical words and psychological slang. And you can see from the following list just how easily confusing jargon can be developed. Techniques of NLP such as Collapsing Anchors, Visual Squash, Six Step Reframing, Visual Kinesthetic Dissociation, Change Personal History, Belief Change, Reimprinting were all derived from applying models. The practical application of all these techniques to selling is explained in this book using plain lucid english. Few NLP authors avoid this 'psycho-babble' and the subject can seem more complicated than it is because of your unfamiliarity with a lot of the vocabulary. As in most technical fields, students who have not yet mastered it are often keen to overuse jargon in order to impress the uninitiated. If you have been put off NLP because of this in the past, you will particularly enjoy the several reads you will inevitably have of this book.

$\overline{\underline{2}}$

How To Win Business By Body Talk Rapport

A. What Exactly Is Rapport?

- A state between two or more people that precedes influence.
- Sharing a 'personal chemistry' with your customer.
- A co-operative relationship.
- Being on the same wavelength as your customer.
- Being in tune with each other.
- Seeing things the same way.
- Having something in common.
- A like-mindedness.

Rapport is the ability to enter someone else's world so that they feel that you understand them, that you have a strong common bond. It is the ability to go fully from your perception of the world to theirs. When this sympathetic relationship or understanding is established, then an environment of trust, confidence and participation is developed.

B. What Can You Do To Create Rapport?

Having something in common – it is as simple as that. This requires a flexible attitude to leave your world and enter somebody else to create rapport. The biggest barrier is thinking that other people look at the world in the same way you do. There is no right way to view the world, hence the saying 'The customer is always right'. If there was, it would not be relevant. Rapport is about having a common view, not a right one.

If you are flexible you can develop rapport with everybody. If you find yourself up against what appears to be resistance, this is your signal to be flexible and try a different tack. Before the end of this chapter you will have gone a long way to mastering these skills. At this point your mastery will only be developed by 'going live' – practising your skills and observing the results you attain. This will lead to habits being formed. At this point you will find it difficult not to develop near instant rapport with everyone you meet.

When people are in rapport they match each other's behaviour at various levels; the opposite is also true. When people are not in rapport they mismatch at various levels. Some of these levels are more significant than others; this is discussed in the next chapter.

Mastering the skill of building rapport requires the ability to be sensitive and observant to information given by the client, and then to use this information by taking action, being flexible and adjusting your response accordingly. Once you have been taught the techniques mastery depends on your ability to perceive other people's postures, gestures and speech patterns and then the elegance in which you can match them.

> *When people think similar they look similar.*
> *When people look similar they think similar.*

C. Analysis Of Influence

In Chapter 1, I referred to the relative influence of the three ways in which we communicate. This shows that establishing a good rapport with body language will be far easier than achieving it with words. Most of us, however, rely on words to develop this common bond and are more adept at it, despite the fact that developing a common bond with body talk is so simple and so powerful. These relative percentages of influence are so critical I would like to stress them again using two illustrations.

1. *55% body language,* 38% tonality, words 7%

2. The difference in influences between the written word and something said face to face can be represented as follows:

Alex, will you come here please.

Written   <   ***words***   >
Face To Face <   ***BODY LANGUAGE***   >*<words>*<*tonality*>

D. Posture Pacing

As you now know there is much more for the receiver to perceive from a given communication than the communicator can know. The notion that there are large portions of our communicated behaviour unavailable to ourselves, yet revealed to the world, can be disconcerting. However carefully we might choose our words the rest of our behaviour speaks most eloquently to the knowledgeable receiver.

Mirroring is not the same as mimicry. Mimicry is exaggeration of a behavioural feature. Mirroring is the subtle, behavioural reflection of the meaningful, unconscious communications each of us offers to the attentive receiver. Mirroring at first can sometimes feel awkward, even manipulative. It soon becomes unconscious and respectful.

The level of rapport you establish with someone is determined by your ability to pace them. Pacing means getting in rhythm with that person. You communicate with someone through body language the second you meet them. You cannot not influence them even if you remain quiet. It only takes a matter of seconds to establish rapport.

Modern psychology has now firmly established that conscious or unconscious pacing – i.e. matching of patterns – is what determines the state of rapport. Most sales people who call on me don't do this –

they operate in their own patterns of behaviour. When they do develop rapport it is by accident.

When you match body language as well as developing rapport, something else of value happens. As our brain and body are part of one system, by matching you will also be accessing the same parts of your brain as they are. This will give you some surprisingly accurate intuitive thoughts as to what they are thinking, what they will do next and how they may react to any proposal. Even better news, this will come to you unconsciously – no effort other than the 'matching' is required. So, go with your instincts: it is based on a lot more reasoning than you realise and will usually be correct. Like a lot of things in this book, you may find this hard to believe without the evidence of personal experience. So, please experiment and see what you find.

E. Establishing Face To Face Rapport

We know that 55% of communication is by body talk. So where do you think the greatest potential is for establishing rapport?

Face-to-face rapport is most effectively achieved by 'matching'. The main aspects of matching body language comprise the following:

- Posture
- Orientation
- Weight distribution
- Gestures (arms, hands, legs, and feet)
- Facial expression
- Eye contact
- Rate of blinking
- Breathing
- Head tilting
- Eye squinting
- Flicks of the eyebrows

When you use the technique of matching, your clients will have the subjective experience of being really understood. After all, you are speaking their body language. You cannot verbally talk your way out of problems you body talk yourself into. You can, however, behave your way out of problems you talk yourself into.

After a short period of time in observer's position, you will notice that people instinctively mirror each other as they develop rapport. You can now begin to do so deliberately to achieve specific outcomes. Start by mirroring just one aspect of another person's behaviour while talking to them. When this is easy and becomes second nature, add another match – such as arm movements – while talking, until you are mirroring without thinking about it.

The more you practise the more you will become aware of the rhythms that you and others generate. Notice the degree to which couples are out of 'sync' when they are miscommunicating, in contrast to when they are doing well with one another.

Beware of attaching 'labels' to body language. Different body posture changes can mean different things for different people. You must first get into their world and then you will realise what a particular body posture means for them.

Remember that the brain and body are intimately connected. Neurology and physiology are directly related. In other words, when you move in unison with someone you are accessing the same parts of your brain as they are theirs – this is why rapport is created. More than rapport, and as you become successful at making the distinctions, you will almost always know more about your prospect's continuing experience than the prospect's themselves are consciously aware of.

F. Matching Breathing

Many people find the concept of matching breathing difficult, when they first learn of it. But consider this: the human body requires the supply of three key resources in order to maintain life – food, water and air. If you fast and deny yourself food, you will probably last for between three and six months. If you fast by cutting out water you will probably live for six to eight days. If you hold your breath you are unlikely to live as long as six to eight minutes. The point is that air is the most crucial thing to the body, not food and water. Eastern mystics have always been aware of this and any book on Yoga will teach you a range of breathing exercises that will better utilise this resource in the body.

Our breathing rate is part of the same system as our pulse, blinking and a whole range of bodily processes. By matching breathing you are immediately setting up what is known technically as a biofeedback loop and lock straight in to somebody's internal world. I like to explain it in terms of tuning in to their frequency.

Calibrating a person's breathing becomes easier with practice and training. It is hard to notice without training. Some people breathe so strongly it is quite clear; in others you can detect a slight movement up and down of their shoulders relative to a fixed point behind. Some people sigh frequently, which gives the pattern. People are, of course, breathing out while they are talking. If you want to develop your skill at this technique get two friends to help you. Have one of them stand behind the other who is sitting. Standing behind is the best point to observe breathing. Have this person do nothing but observe the breathing of the seated person from close quarters and to show it to you by raising their hand up and down with large sweeps in time with the breathing. Observing this you can pace the hand movements easily and talk in the same patterns. Practise at least a dozen times like this in half-hour sessions and you will start to find that it is becoming habitual. Taking away the support then will not make any difference as you have trained your sensory antenna to a new level.

Be careful of the now outdated 'interpretive model' of body language that basically says '*x* posture means *y*'. This does not tell you how to utilise this knowledge with reference to your objectives. If somebody's fist is banging on the desk it is probably a fair guess that they are angry. However, when we are trying to interpret subtle postures or changes in posture you can make sweeping generalisations but they are not going to be true for everybody. By pacing you can calibrate for the individual. In other words, when Harry folds his arms it means that he is resistant. When Mary folds her arms it means that she is cold. When John folds his arms it is because he is conscious of his paunch and wishes to cover it. By pacing we are avoiding the risk of being wrong and we respect everybody as an individual.

Have you ever observed total strangers at a football match? As the game progresses they sway together, applaud, jump up, chant, cheer and boo together. The fans on both sides do everything in unison with their fellow fans and at different times to the opponent fans. They are establishing and developing a deeper rapport with each other while moving further away from the facing fans. Bad behaviour when the two conflicting groups meet is not so much surprising as inevitable!

G. How Do You Know When You Are In Rapport?

Simply, when you change your posture and the other party then mirrors you. Next time you are out, observe the postures people adopt in relation to who they are with or talking to. See if your own evidence supports the idea that when people are in rapport their posture is similar. And conversely, when people are not, are their postures clearly different? When in rapport what do you find happens if one changes posture?

Watch people in a restaurant, a pub, wine bar or night club – perhaps a couple out together, or a sales representative entertaining a client. When they are in rapport do they tend to retain eye contact, nod simultaneously, heads moving in similar ways, shoulders at the same angle, arms in the same posture? It is essential that you go out and observe this for yourself. If you do, you will create a belief change and you will find your patterns beginning to automatically change to gain rapport.

Posture pacing someone means first noticing how they use their body language. It may be a clap of the hands, a tap on the desk or drawing imaginary pictures in front of themselves. If you describe your points back to them, drawing them out in this way, it will be meaningful in the customer's world. It gets your message through in their language. Some may consider this manipulative – I consider it service. I think that it is the salesman's duty to talk the future client's language and develop rapport in any way he can. Have you ever entered a showroom and been ignored, and walked out? Then gone into another showroom, met a professional who developed rapport and got into your way of seeing the world? From this information he clearly explained to you the benefits of a particular product that suited you. He then closed the deal. That is what I want, in fact that is what most people want from a salesman. I enjoy spending money and I want to buy things that are going to add value to my life. I consider it exploitative when this is not done and I just come up against pushiness, pressure, lack of integrity or just not being listened to.

I am not saying that you have to mirror every slight movement; it need not be so literal that it is obvious. Posture pacing is an unconscious mind communication. Unless we deliberately set out to do so, we do not consciously notice the body talk of others. Ask yourself what the postures were on the last three meetings that you had. I suspect that you had to really think about it. Now, during a sales presentation you have a lot to think about. Matching body language while thinking about what to say, handling objections and listening attentively is rather a lot to do. In fact your conscious mind (left brain) can only process up to nine pieces of information at a time. Clearly a lot has to be filtered out and concentration has to be placed on the most critical parts. The way to do this is to develop your body language rapport skills to a level where it is carried out unconsciously. In other words, every time you meet someone you automatically match them without realising you are doing it. That way your conscious mind is left free to pay attention and listen.

H. A Practical Illustration

Once I accompanied a colleague on a sales presentation to pitch for an assignment to recruit a Financial Director for a major manufacturer of aircraft components in Surrey. My colleague took the lead and I supported him. Not having to concentrate on what I was going to say next I had the opportunity to concentrate on what I could observe.

I watched every movement and paced it. I moved forward, moved my arms and even matched his breathing. I then tried leading the client to a more relaxed posture by sitting back and slowing my breathing rate. The client followed. I started to smile increasingly. He followed. Bear in mind that he never directly looked at me during the presentation as he was concentrating on the dialogue he was having with my partner. We had established an *empathy bond* on a totally non-verbal level. The point is that non-verbal rapport is all that you need. When you have rapport you do not have to keep agreeing with the client – you can disagree verbally and still maintain rapport and your differing views will be considered openly.

We got the deal there and then against stiff competition. That is one of the things I like about maintaining rapport through body language alone. You are not tempted to agree when you do not in fact agree and still know that you are not risking the deal.

The more you pace non-verbally the more you will notice how different everybody's posture and movements are. Remember, by pacing their physiology you will also be accessing the same neurological circuits in your brain. This means that you will start receiving 'intuitions' about what he or she is going to do or say next. You will literally be getting into their world more and more. This is paying respect, and not forcing your 'model of the world' on them. Only when you have entered their world will you know what is best for the future client. Establishing this, pointing it out and then supplying it is professional selling. Establishing it and realising that what you offer is not the best solution for the prospect and suggesting alternatives is professional selling. Pretending that your goods and services match his requirements when you do not believe it, is negative manipulation and unethical. No respectable company will support this. Few customers will supply references, referrals or future orders. Thinking long-term while working under extreme short-term pressures (targets) is one of the things that separates the very top performing sales people from the average.

I. Leading

When you have rapport the next stage is to lead the prospect to where you want him to go. Now you go ahead changing their behaviour by getting them to follow your lead. You can test if you have rapport by changing your body language in some way – such as crossed-legged to uncrossed – and seeing if they follow. They are now receptive to what you want to say and you can lead the conversation. You can proceed to find their needs and then match your products or services to them. Because you are in a heightened state of rapport, repetitive test closing will be unnecessary.

3

How To Win Business By Vocal Rapport

A. Rapport On The Telephone

"Our quality of after-sales service is excellent."

Telephone: < *Words* ><   *Tonality*   >

On the telephone, the study previously referred to concluded that 84% of the message is communicated through how you speak (tonality) and only 16% through words. Let us therefore look at tonality first. Like body language rapport is developed by matching, so what can we match?

Your tone of voice – i.e. your rhythm, speed, timbre, pitch, volume, enthusiasm, etc. – when matched will develop near instant rapport, irrespective of what is being said. Clearly what is being said can enhance or work against this 'tonal' rapport, but the effect is minimal. The unconscious mind, where the decisions are made, will pick up everything in your tone, although it may not communicate its knowledge to the conscious mind. That is why this is so hard to believe. You are considering it consciously.

It follows that telephone selling based upon scripts could potentially be improved six times. There is a lot more to it than 'Smile As You Dial'. In fact, that approach on many occasions will lose you sales. However NLP techniques can be learnt and applied by anyone, guaranteeing near instant rapport. When this happens typical sales staff start to look forward to telephone canvassing and the constant 'buzz' of success that it brings them. After applying these techniques you will find that you change excuses into results.

Taking the prospect's words, attaching *your* meaning to them translating them into the language *you* use, and communicating from your linguistic style, are all steps that are arbitrary on your part, and are quite likely to lead to confusion.

Using the language of your client is the best way to have an impact on him. Words represent experience, and even though we use a common language, our experiences are necessarily different. If you use somebody's own words back to them they will instinctively feel that they have been understood.

Imagine you are about to call someone. Unknown to you, they have had a whole month of bad news and to top it all their wife has just rung and said that the house is flooded from a burst water main. Having just finished a book called 'Smile As You Dial', you open: 'Hi, good morning, isn't it wonderful? Hey, you sound down, what's the matter? Cheer up, I'm sure everything is going to work out great.' All said with a lively enthusiastic tonality. Their reaction would be one of the following:

1. Totally uplifted by this completely positive person, forget their problems and consider placing a big order; or

2. Be totally wound up, and wonder why it is always *them* who have these problems – why it is *them* who always get these phone calls. Then tell you to get lost, politely.

Now I would like to think I am in category 1, but I know that I am in category 2.

Can I suggest that when on the phone (as opposed to face-to-face, when body talk will immediately indicate the mood of the prospect) you match everything you can – words *and* tone, remembering that getting the tone right will have a far greater effect than the words. However, practise one thing at a time. In your next ten calls, speak back to the caller in the same tone of voice that they use – fast/slow, enthusiastic/calm, changing tempo/monotone, changing pitch/ constant pitch, etc. If you are still not convinced try mismatching some calls and see how much rapport develops.

In tonal matching you can find yourself emotionally pacing. You call a person in a very bad mood. They say: 'Oh dear, I suppose you're looking for an order. We are totally overwhelmed here today.' You respond: 'Oh dear, what exactly is the problem?' in a similar tone of voice. You experience the emotion of the moment with them, whatever that emotion happens to be. Matching a strong emotion gets you strong rapport fast.

Now think about this. Think of a time recently in you life when you have found yourself with somebody who was emotional, positively or negatively. Remember how you reacted to them and what effect this had on them. If you are still not convinced try mismatching and watch the result. The next time you are with someone who is angry, or 'throwing a wobbly', say 'Calm down', or 'Stop Shouting', in a really calm voice. In my experience this throws oil on the fire. Next time say in a matching tone, 'Oh no, I can really understand why you are angry', and then lead on to calmer grounds.

B. Listening In On A World Of Difference

Okay, so it's not what you say but how you say it. Have you noticed that people speak at different speeds? We speak at the rate which is comfortable for us. In fact, we change our speed due to changes in our internal state. However, we all have a 'default 'rate that we are most comfortable with. If we are comfortable speaking at this rate it follows that we would find it easier to listen to someone speaking at the same speed. Have you ever had the experience of listening to someone who talks very fast and finding it difficult to communicate with them?

Or the opposite – somebody who talks very slowly and you become frustrated, urging them to speed up. Well, if you want to get on to somebody's frequency fast you can do so immediately by talking at the same speed as them.

Similarly, people talk at different volumes. We can even make sweeping generalisations by nationality. How would you compare the volume of normal speech of a German and a Frenchman? The same rules apply. We all believe that the 'normal' volume for speech is the one that we happen to be talking at. Therefore if you wish to get on to your future client's frequency try speaking at the volume he does.

Incidentally, when you are on someone's frequency, in rapport, they are unlikely to notice you pacing them. To them you are talking normally. When I am leading seminars I always change my tone of voice to match that of a person asking a question. Sometimes other delegates notice the change but the person who asked the question never has, even when discussing tone. Try it yourself and see (and hear) what you find.

Always remember that non-verbal pacing has more influence than tone and language combined. If the prospect talks about his hobby of train-spotting, which you find thoroughly boring, that's great. Non-verbally pace and concentrate on listening to every word and calculate how it can be utilised. You will be developing a deep rapport without saying a word – gaining valuable information on the client's needs, style and interests which may be used later in achieving the required result.

C. High-Level Pacing

At the highest level of our mind are our beliefs, values and identity. Pacing at this level can be very profound indeed as these areas are by definition the most important part of us, determining our behaviour in any situation. As they are so important, pacing someone else in these areas might cause internal conflict with your own beliefs, value and identity. Let us have a brief look at each in turn.

Identity

I am...

I am a Christian; a Scotsman; a man; a top-class sales professional; an ideal father and husband....

What identity or identities are important for you?

Values

Trying to buy business by offering bribes, even subtle ones, usually conflicts and breaks rapport at the level of values. In parts of the Middle East and Asia bribery is an accepted way of doing business. If you do not pay (what we would label bribes) no business will be transacted. In England this is not acceptable behaviour, although the business lunch or the occasional promotional gift is. A manager who is treated to lunch by a sales representative would not be considered corrupt. Where the line is drawn is purely a matter of values.

Beliefs

'You get what you pay for.' Or, 'Watch the pennies and the pounds will look after themselves.'

These types of beliefs tend to be deep and thus are difficult to change. I therefore suggest matching them; show how your proposal conforms to the belief and is in accordance with it.

Corporate culture is another high level of rapport where one can identify with the group. Those of you who have teenage children will know just how powerful this can be. Or is it just coincidence that they happen to like the same clothes, foods, places all at the same time! Group behavioural studies have long shown us how powerful peer pressure to conform in a group can be. When the informal rules for conformity are established anyone not abiding with them will simply not fit in. Corporate culture manifests itself in terms of dress, style of suit, tie, etc., attitudes, how superiors are addressed (Sir, Mr McMillan or Alex). In the army calling your immediate superior by his first name won't go down well; in an advertising agency it would. One might expect more formality in a firm of accountants in the City than in the same firm's office in the provinces. The point is this: more important than dressing as smartly as you can (and sometimes contrary to it), you should match your style of dress to that of the organisation you are visiting.

In China and Japan it is customary for all staff to start the day by singing the company song. What a way to get the team in total rapport, identity, values, beliefs, physiology, tone and language all at the same time!

The business lunch is a good opportunity to gain some very easy rapport-enhancing points. Have you ever gone to lunch with someone and had a pint of lager while they drank Perrier water? You are out of frequency with that person. You then order steak pie, chips and beans and they have a cheese sandwich. The disrapport that something like this creates is quite strong. People have a natural tendency to feel happy when they are like you. Have you heard the conversations of people in the bar discussing food or wine? Notice the amount of times you hear 'I will if you will'. This might mean wine or not with the meal. Now, armed with this knowledge, ask your future client what they would like to drink first and match it. Find out what they are eating first and order something similar. This will get you far closer to getting their business than, for example, trying to impress them by insisting that you pay.

In my previous partnership we had offices in the City and in Sussex. A client lunch in the City was typically a bottle of quality wine in a classy restaurant. A client lunch in Sussex was typically a beer and a pie in a pub. In the City clients want to get straight down to business. In Sussex clients want to get to know you better and do not wish to be hurried. If there is so much difference in behaviour within 30 miles, imagine the variety of someone who transacts business internationally! Find out what they would prefer (all you need do is ask), and be flexible in your style to match theirs.

Bear in mind that your future clients cannot not communicate.

Therefore there is always enough communication to develop rapport on and the only situation where you cannot develop rapport is when one of you turns their back and exits.

Bear in mind that the rapport techniques in this and the previous chapters have been developed from NLP practitioners – a large range of communicators enjoying formidable results. When practised and developed to a high degree these advanced, yet simple rapport skills produce incredible results in seconds.

D. The Hierarchy Of Rapport

********* DEEP CORE *********
Identity
Values
Beliefs

****** PHYSIOLOGY ******
Posture
Breathing
Blinking
Nodding

**** TONALITY ****
Volume
Pitch
Rhythm
Speed

** LANGUAGE **
Buzzwords
Predicates
Phrases
Metaphors
Sensory Language System

E. Moving On Once Rapport Is Established

Once you have rapport, and that need only be a minute, you are in a position to lead to wherever you want to go. You are 'hooking them' on to you with your pacing. You are respecting their present world by talking to them in it. Following your lead, they will increasingly adapt your tone of voice after you speak. If this does not happen you have not established a strong enough state of rapport. No problem, just go back to stage one. When you have a high level of rapport, the client (for he will no longer be a prospect) is likely to say something along the lines of: 'You know, you and I are a lot alike,' or 'We are kindred spirits'.

If rapport is about getting on the same frequency as your future client, the next stage is to listen, gather information, then lead the conversation into matching client needs to what you have to offer and finally, of course, to close the deal. You lead the conversation by well directed questions (covered in Chapter 5). Then ask for the business.

4

Talking Your Future Client's Language

A. What Influences You?

Complete the following questionnaire, coding as follows.

> 4 = Closest to describing you
> 3 = Next best
> 2 = Not particularly you
> 1 = Least like you

Code

1. I make important decisions based on:
   Gut level feelings.. __
   Which way sounds best .... __
   What looks best to me .... __
   Precise review and study of the issues.............................. __

2. During an argument, I am most likely to be influenced by:
   The other person's tone of voice .... __
   Whether or not I can see the other person's argument ...... __
   The logic of the other person's points................................. __
   Being in touch with the issues .... __

3. I am happiest when:
   I am listening to music .... __
   I have balanced my personal budget .... __
   Going for a walk on a sunny day .... __
   Watching a good movie .... __

4. My main motivation to exercise and keep fit is:
   It would make me feel better.. __
   It would make me look better .... __
   A class with music to supply rhythm................................. __
   Improved performance in my career................................... __

5. If I bought a pet it would be because:
   They are warm and cuddly .... __
   Their sound is very welcoming .... __
   They look just lovely .... __
   I can make money from breeding them .... __

6. Are you more receptive to people who:
   Are very precise in their communication........................... __
   Have a pleasant friendly voice .... __
   Dress well and look smart... __
   Give you a firm handshake .... __

7. I communicate how I am at any time by:
   The way I dress and look .... __
   The feelings I share with friends....................................... __
   The words I choose... __
   The tone of my voice... __

8 It is easiest for me to:
   Find the ideal volume and tuning on a stereo system .... __
   Select the most intellectually relevant point .... __
   Select the most comfortable furniture .... __
   Select rich, attractive, colour combinations....................... __

9 I am very:

    Responsive to the decorations in a room .... __

    Tuned to the sounds of my surroundings .... __

    Adept at making sense of new facts and data .... __

    Sensitive to clothes on my body .... __

10 When I buy my dream car I will be most influenced by:

    How it looks – colour, design, etc. .... __

    The sensation of speed from behind the wheel .... __

    The quality of the stereo and quietness of engine .... __

    The best deal I can get .... __

Copy your answers onto the following table:

1 – F __	2 – S __	3 – S __	4 – F __	5 – F __
– S __	– P __	– L __	– P __	– S __
– P __	– L __	– F __	– S __	– P __
– L __	– F __	– P __	– L __	– L __

6 – L __	7 – P __	8 – S __	9 – P __	10 – P __
– S __	– F __	– L __	– S __	– F __
– P __	– L __	– F __	– L __	– S __
– F __	– S __	– P __	– F __	– L __

Now transfer your scores to the following matrix:

Question	Pictures (P)	Feelings (F)	Logic (L)	Sounds (S)
1.				
2.				
3.				
4.				
5.				
6.				
7.				
8.				
9.				
10.				
TOTAL				

(Note that the smell and taste sensory languages are not separately included in this test as they are considered less significant, and are often included in 'Feelings' for these purposes)

My language preference order is:

First   =

Second =

Third   =

Fourth =

B. Are We Talking The Same Language?

Four salesman met on a sales training course and after talking realised that they had each just come back from holiday. They related their holidays to each other, as represented below. Which one appeals to you the most?

The first salesman, Harry, said that his resort was beautiful. There were panoramic views of an attractive coastline and it was sunny every day. The sea was a deep shade of green, contrasting with a picturesque sky of light blue. The town itself was attractive with lots to see of interest. Harry took his wife and said that when they returned they both looked very good with attractive tans. He imagined that they would be going back there next year.

John spent all of his holiday enjoying various sports –particularly water sports, which he described as giving you a tremendous feeling with the sun on your face, the wind in your hair and an exhilaration from speed felt all over the body. He went dancing most evenings and ate and drank copiously.

George had chosen his resort after careful analysis of the alternatives to ensure best value for money. He reckoned that his chosen resort offered the best all-round package and he was not disappointed. He made a clear plan of what he wanted to do, which involved a great deal of diverse activities. He studied all the tours available to avoid repetition and scheduled them in with periods of complete rest and relaxation.

Peter said that his resort was lively and they spent most evenings listening to local musicians with the background sound of the surf breaking. The traffic was a bit noisy but the hotel was situated in a quiet part of the town. He chose this holiday because of a friend's recommendation, which was supported by what he was told by the travel agent.

Now the above holidays could all be the same resort. Harry clearly prefers pictures, John feelings, George logic,and Peter sounds. The one that appealed to you the most gives a good orientation as to your preferred sensory system.

Sometimes we do not seem to be speaking the same language.

Good communication skills bridge these differences and provide flexibility, which is the mother of influence.

C. A Closer Look At 'Native' Language

Our experiences are structured in terms of our senses. When we think or process information internally we either use one of the sensory languages or the one non-sensory language which we call the logic mode. These five different languages can be directly compared to spoken languages, such as French, German, Spanish, Greek or Japanese. If you were selling to a Japanese you would probably do better by speaking Japanese and even better using the style, customs and manner of a Japanese. This way you will literally be speaking his language and therefore develop rapport and communicate far easier with him.

The same principle applies to the 'languages of the mind' and you are already conversant in all of them – we all speak all of these languages some of the time. However, for most people one language is predominant, and doing nothing more than talking to someone in their preferred language will virtually guarantee you getting your message through. The languages are:

- Pictures
- Feelings
- Logic
- Sounds
- Smell/taste

There are now two simple things to do:

1. Establish which language somebody is predominantly using. This can be done by any one of the following methods, using the others for confirmation.

   (a) Listen to the words and phrases repeatedly used.

(b) Their body shape is a major indicator.
(c) Certain involuntary eye movements.
(d) Breathing patterns.

2. Talk to them in that language.

(a) Use the words and phrase of that language, particularly the same ones.
(b) Mirror their physiology, which will be strongly influenced by their 'native' language.
(c) Show 'pictures people' things, (brochures, charts, references, reports, pictures etc); talk to 'sounds people' about what other customers have said. Let 'feelings people' touch your product and try it out; explain to 'logic people' the arguments in favour of your products.

As an interesting exercise to illustrate the need to be completely flexible, imagine that you are a car salesman and consider how you may differently approach each type of customer.

D. 'Pictures' Language Customers

Vocabulary

Look	Picture	Bright	Outlook	Focus
Image	Dim View	Black	White	Colour
Hazy	Insight	Vivid	Glowing	Scene
Blank	Visualise	Dim	Dark	Clear
Luminous	Perspective	Vision	Shine	Shady
Reflect	Gleam	Golden	Opaque	Eye
Transparent	Translucent	Reflect	Imagine	Dream
Focus	Hindsight	Horizon	Illusion	

Phrases/Metaphors

I cannot face it.
Looking at the big picture.
It's not exactly black and white to me.
I need to distance myself from the problem.
He's had a colourful past.
He has a sunny disposition.
Looks alright to me.
I cannot seem to focus on what you are saying.
That puts a bit more light on it.
That's brightened up my day.
It all seems very hazy.
I see what you mean.
I want a different perspective.
Let us look at this closely.
I can picture what you are saying.
I can see right through your argument.
Show me what you mean.
Things are looking up.
It appears that you are right.
Seeing eye to eye.
Turn a blind eye.

Exercise

Construct five questions to ask 'pictures' people.

1.

2.

3.

4.

5.

E. 'Feelings' Language Customers

Vocabulary

Touch	Move	Pressure	Handle	Loose
Thrust	Texture	Grasp	Weight	Smooth
Pushy	Rub	Tight	Contact	Sticky
Shrug	Solid	Warm	Cold	Tepid
Itching	Flow	Tackle	Turn	Uptight
Tickle	Tight	Firm	Lift	Sensitive
Hassle	Hold	Soft	Tired	Sharp
Support	Touch Base			

Phrases/Metaphors

I am ready to tackle this head on.
I've got a good feel about this.
He needs to get a grip on his results.
He is as solid as a rock.
It is a rather sticky situation.
I need a concrete proposal.
You hurt his feelings.
A cool customer.
Can you give me a hand.
Things just seemed to flow smoothly.
He rubs me up the wrong way.
That company needs to pull itself together.
I can grasp what you are saying.
Can you hold on a minute.
I feel it in my bones.
One step at a time.
Hot-headed.
A pat on the back
Boils down to.
Tied up.

Exercise

Construct five questions to ask 'feelings' people.

1.

2.

3.

4.

5.

F. 'Logic' Language Customers

Vocabulary

Logic	Analyse	Think	Review	Balancing
Measure	Calculate	Assess	Reason	Sense
Judgement	Validate	Breakdown	Estimate	Dissect
Enquire	Examine	Investigate	Scrutinise	Rational
Systematic	Arrange	Testing	Sift	Evaluate
Believe	Conceive	Conclude	Consider	Judge
Reckon	Suppose	Surmise	Cogitate	Deliberate
Muse	Ponder	Criticise	Study	Survey
Compute	Figure	Gauge	Work Out	Mentality
Understand	Perceive	Basis	Remember	Critique
Conclude	Decide	Number	Conjecture	Guess
Rank	Know	Notice	Explain	Common sense

Phrases/Metaphors

I would like to think about it.
Consider it done.
Let me think about it.
Seems logical to me.

I reckon your right.
I understand what you mean.
I guess it adds up to a good deal.

Exercise

Construct five questions to ask 'logic' people.

1.

2.

3.

4.

5.

G. 'Sounds' Language Customers

Vocabulary

Say	Question	Click	Rhythm	Chatter
Tinkle	Sing	Melody	Tone	Patter
Hearsay	Drum	Chirpy	Loud	Harmony
Deaf	Language	Speech	Tune	Ring
Clash	Call	Dumb	Hear	Wavelength
Dissonant	Tell	Talk	Unheard of	Monotonous

Phrases/Metaphors

We are on the same wavelength.
Speaking the same language.
Tune into this.
I hear what you are saying.
Music to my ears.

I like what you are saying.
Lost for words.
Living in harmony.
Talking gobbledygook.
Noise in the system.
Quiet as a mouse.
Sounds good to me.
Turn a deaf ear.
Tone it down.
Rings a bell.
Strikes a chord.
Struck dumb.
Calling the tune.
Loud and clear.
I have heard a whisper.
I keep telling him.
It's come to a screeching halt.
Rumour has it.

Exercise

Construct five questions to ask 'sounds' people.

1.

2.

3.

4.

5.

H. 'Smells / Tastes' Language Customers

Vocabulary

Scent	Whiff	Sweet	Bitter	Reek
Fishy	Flavour	Appetite	Nosey	Aroma
Savour	Gorge	Fresh	Stinks	Chew
Swallow	Bouquet	Acrid	Bland	Spicy
Smell	Fragrant	Bite	Juicy	Sniff
Crisp	Luscious	Nibble		

Phrases/Metaphors

Seems a bit fishy to me.
The sweet taste/smell of success.
He is stinking rich.
Taking a sugar-coated pill.
He has a good nose for business.
He's all sour grapes.
It makes the spice of life.
He has bitten off more than he can chew.
I'd like to get a bite of that apple.
He came out of that deal smelling of roses.
Our northern branch is a peach operation.
I need to get to the meat of the proposal.
I'd like a better price for starters.
Too many cooks spoil the broth.
If you do not like the heat get out of the kitchen.

Exercise

Construct five questions to ask 'smells/tastes' people.

1.

2.

3.

4.

5.

I. It's All In The Eyes!

When we are not consciously looking at something we move our eyes according to what language we are operating internally. There are exceptions to this rule but they are rare. (The main exceptions are left-handed people. In their case the opposite direction is usually found.)

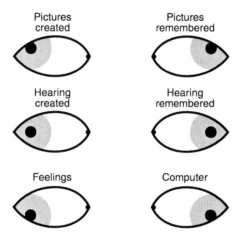

Figure 1. Looking At Someone

The central position usually means that the person is accessing different 'languages' at the same time. Remember that this is a generalisation and it is always best to calibrate for the individual. Also, these movements are unconscious and indicate where the 'unconscious' mind is – the conscious mind could be elsewhere.

J. Where Do The Eyes Go?

Put the following questions to at least three people and, without telling them what you are doing, record where their eyes go. The response types and the predicted eye positions are as follows:

	Left	Right
Up	Pictures Remembered (PR)	Pictures Created (PC)
Central	Hearing Remembered (HR)	Hearing Created (HC)
Down	Computer (C)	Feelings (F)

Questions

What does your house look like? (PR)
　　　　Eyes: Up/Central/Down Left/Right

What does your favourite Disney character look like? (PR)
　　　　Eyes: Up/Central/Down Left/Right

What would your dream car look like? (PC)
　　　　Eyes: Up/Central/Down Left/Right

Picture yourself driving a red Ferrari? (PC)
　　　　Eyes: Up/Central/Down Left/Right

SR What was the last sentence you spoke? (SR)
　　　　Eyes: Up/Central/Down Left/Right

What does Donald Duck sound like? (SR)
　　　　Eyes: Up/Central/Down Left/Right

Imagine the voice of your last prospect? (SC)
　　　　Eyes: Up/Central/Down Left/Right

What would I sound like talking Japanese? (SC)
Eyes: Up/Central/Down Left/Right

What does 3 + 12 - 7 + 5 make? (C)
Eyes: Up/Central/Down Left/Right

What does £11 + VAT total? (C)
Eyes: Up/Central/Down Left/Right

What is toothache like? (F)
Eyes: Up/Central/Down Left/Right

What part of you gets hottest quickest in a sauna? (F)
Eyes: Up/Central/Down Left/Right

K. Typical Characteristics Of 'Native' Language Speakers.

Preference - Pictures

These speakers' voices are often high-pitched and slightly breathless. They tend to breathe high in the chest. They often have tension in the neck and shoulders. Voice tempo is often quite quick.

'Pictures' people seldom get lost; if they are in a place once, they will remember the area and find their way back. They typically have photographic memories and can vividly retrieve past scenes with ease.

Physical characteristics may be summarised as follows: eyes up, head up, frequent blinking, even closing of eyes. They tend to be thinner and dress well.

Preference - Feelings

'Feelings' people breathe low down in the belly, and accordingly their voices tend to be deeper than the other categories. They tend to speak slowly often with spaces or gaps. Their eyes tend down to the right. They often love sports and use gestures a lot.

Preference - Logic

'Logic' people do not trust their basic experiences. They trust the words that describe the experiences instead. This gives them a cautious outlook, as they search for the perfect description.

Preference - Sounds

Not as common as the above three. They often speak well and rhythmically. They are constantly talking to themselves in internal dialogue. In fact they are often hard to close on as they won't turn off the internal dialogue. They tend to breathe in the middle of the chest. This gives them a rhythmic tempo. As you can imagine they like listening to music or attending concerts.Their eyes tend to be level left and right. They will often hum or whistle

Think of people that you deal with a lot. Which categories do they fit into?

L. Examples Of Multi-Lingual Sales Lines

Pictures

If I could *show* you an *attractive* (benefit), you would want at least to *look* at it, wouldn't you?
Imagine in your *mind's eye* owning this product.
Can you *see* what I am getting at?
Can you *visualise* the benefits of this product?
Can I *focus* you on these particular features?
You should *see* this as a *golden* opportunity.
Does this *reflect* your requirements?

Feelings

If this *feels* good to you, I can *pull* some strings for delivery Monday.
Can you get a *feel* for what I am saying?
Can I *touch base* with you next week?
We have to *stick* to the label price on this one.
It takes all the *hassle* out of buying.

Logic

Considering the arguments, what do you *think*?
Do you want me to *investigate* further?
What do you *reckon*?
It is the only *logical* choice.
The *figures add up*, don't they?

Sounds

If I could *tell* you a way in which you could benefit, you would at least want to *hear* about it, wouldn't you?
How does that *sound*?
Listen to this *quote* from John Smith of ABC Systems.
Are we on the same *wavelength*?
Tell me what you *think*?
Have you changed your *tune*?

Smells/Tastes

Sniffing out opportunities.
Taste of his own medicine.
The deal on the new lease *stinks*.
Losing that contract was *rotten* luck.
That way of doing business I find *distasteful*.

M. A Second Look At What Influences You

Write down five sentences of things that you like or dislike strongly. Be sure to describe exactly what it is that you like or dislike.

1. ....
   ....
   ....

2. ....
   ....
   ....

3. ....
   ....
   ....

4. ....
   ....
   ....

5. ....
   ....
   ....

Now go through the above underlining the Pictures, Feelings, Logic and Sounds words and add them up. Check the results with the test at the beginning of this chapter to confirm your personal profile.

	Pictures	Feelings	Logic	Sounds
Totals				

5

Getting The Right Results By Asking The Right Questions

A. Questioning Techniques

A co-founder of NLP, John Grinder, a Professor Of Linguistics at the University Of California, modelled America's greatest communicators. This included a Dr Milton Erickson, who had revolutionised what had been traditional hypnosis and was President of the American Society for Hypnosis and Hypnotherapy. As a professor of linguistics observing the effects of Erickson's language patterns amazed him. It was later established from modelling top performing sales superstars, that unknowingly these patterns were getting them their exceptional results.

From this and other NLP research there are two major models of language: the Meta model, which is a set of questions that gets straight to the core issues, and the Milton model, used by hypnotists in a pure form to gain access to the unconscious mind. There is nothing I have experienced in linguistic communication as powerful as these two models. The questioning techniques in this chapter have been developed from these original ideas to be of practical use in business.

To learn how to take advantage of these language patterns is like learning to drive a car. You do not need to understand why or how they work to be totally competent using them. You do, however, need someone who can teach you these skills without using jargon, making them practical and of immediate effect to the sales professional in the UK. (It has been quite common in the UK for people with a smattering of knowledge to market themselves as NLP for business trainers, totally convincing their audience that NLP has nothing of substance to offer them.) You then need lots of practice and feedback from your own experience of applying them until they become refined and habitual.

Let us look at how sales staff often dig themselves into a hole with the wrong question.

Salesman:	Would you like to give me an order then?
Future Client:	Thanks for calling but I'll leave it for now.
Salesman:	Can I ask why that is?
Future Client:	Because....

Most sales people regularly ask '*why*' questions, particularly when up against a rejection. This produces in the prospect a virtually automatic response beginning with *because*. That in turn produces all the reasons *why not* to buy. And while the future client is speaking his mental state has gone into 'I do not want to buy' mode, and continually searches for more and more reasons for his decision. This has the effect of making him even more convinced that it was a right decision. Then the salesman produces the 'buts' and starts stressing benefits, sounding more and more desperate as the sale becomes harder and harder to retrieve.

Instead, try opening his mind. Better still, expand it by concentrating on owning your products or enjoying your services. Replace why questions with:

'What do you think would happen if you did buy from us?'
'What is the one thing you need to know in order to be interested?'

These questions will get you out of the ping-pong 'he says, you say' mentality and lead the conversation somewhere fruitful. Try it and see what happens. They may well lead to objections – which is good, as in order to handle objections you first need to establish what they are. From that information you can determine the right key that will let the customer in.

B. Selling Is Simple

I know an office products company that every time it recruits, at the final stage, it sends candidates to a known tough customer. If they succeed and get an order they get the job. Recently they were recruiting and I enquired as to the progress of the candidates.

The first one tried the 'nice guy, I am your friend' approach. He introduced himself, talked around the subject to get the prospect relaxed. When he had accomplished this he asked lots of questions in a very soft way, questions that led the prospect to answers requiring the use of his products as the solution. He was surprised therefore when he gave a closing question that the prospect said: 'Thanks for coming I will bear you in mind when I am next ordering.' He had made the mistake of asking a question beginning 'Why...'. This was, of course, responded to with an answer starting 'Because...', and all the bull**** was vented.

The second salesman had a different approach. He believed all a customer was really interested in was the best possible price. He said hello and went into a presentation emphasising that his quality products were the most competitively priced and that he guaranteed that he would beat any competitor. His closing question was equally straightforward: 'So what do you say?' He got an even more straightforward answer: 'No'. He then re-threw what were to him the unbeatable benefits at the prospect. Alas, to no avail. He left bemused and baffled, believing that a competitor had already got in with better prices.

The third sales representative was a lady who had built a reputation for winning in very difficult situations. She introduced herself and very professionally asked a series of questions eliciting a lot of useful information. She finished with the alternative close: 'Would you prefer delivery on Mondays or Fridays? The prospect used to teach English and immediately recognised the presupposition as a hard selling technique. He replied: 'Would you prefer I turn you down now or at the end of the week?' He'd clearly got her. If she had laughed and admitted her attempt to close, she would still have stood a chance. However, she 'lost her cool' and made fumbled attempts to cover her tactics. 'Sorry, what do you mean... I was just asking... to find out.' She was not convincing.

The fourth sales representative, knowing of the previous candidate's failure, went up to the prospect and said: 'I know that many salesmen have tried to get your business and failed. Can I ask you just one simple question?' 'Yes, go ahead.' 'What would I have to do in order to win your business?' The prospect told him. 'Not try to use any fancy closing techniques to trap me into buying. All I want to see is your products, your prices and to be convinced that I will receive good, honest service.' The representative said: 'Here is a sample of a product.They are £25 each and I will do whatever it takes within my power to keep you as a satisfied customer.' He got the order.

The one right question will have the effect of a cruise missile.
Straight to the target with the desired result.

Unseen by the successful representative, an observer had been watching the discourse and had noticed some absolutely amazing things about the two's body language, postures, tones of voice, words, linguistic patterns and even breathing. He went up to the representative and asked him if he had done this deliberately or by intuition. What do you think?

C. What Can Questions Achieve?

Before you read further, write down twelve potential benefits arising from asking the right questions:

1. ....
2. ....
3. ....
4. ....
5. ....
6. ....
7. ....
8. ....
9. ....
10. ....
11. ....
12. ....

The following is a list of answers produced by a cross-sectional group from a recent seminar. How do they compare to your answers?

Establishing facts
Qualifying potential customers
Establishing requirements
Establishing individual needs
Identifying decision-makers
Identifying decision influencers
Discovering personality type of future client
Establishing size of budget
Establishing price constraints
Establishing the target's position with regard to competitors
Revealing motivation ('hot buttons')
Establishing relationships
Determining whether one-off or ongoing customer potential
Discovering external relationships

Helping to create rapport
Opportunities for listening and observing
Enabling understanding and clarification
Test closing
Closing
Opening
Communicating embedded commands
Tag questions*
Changing customer's 'state of mind'
Establishing presuppositions.

* A tag question makes a statement and then ties your agreement in. Adding a tag question to the end of a statement makes it stronger in the listener's mind. For example:

The products are good, aren't they?
We all like good value, don't we?
Value For Money is important, isn't it?
Speed of delivery is an important issue, isn't it?
The products meet the specification, don't they?

They are best used when reflecting back something that the prospect has said. He cannot therefore disagree and you are creating a run of affirmatives.

Your main task in a sales presentation is to find out how you can help the future client. This you do with questioning, but not any old questions. They have to direct the prospect's mind to where you want to get to – eliciting information and then using this information to open the client's mind to new choices. The real talent, once you have an armoury of precision questions, is to know what questions to ask and clear the fog, red herrings, etc., along the way. This is best done by having a clear outcome in mind before you start. You have to find out what is happening in their mind, not yours. To them this is reality, irrespective of any evidence to the contrary. Don't fall into the trap of making assumptions; instead use the homing questions that I am going to teach you. Your challenge is to elicit clarity through questions and then to make an offer in the client's own language in their own reality.

For example, questions to elicit the real needs of a future client should be something like the following. Notice that they have inbuilt checks that they are the core needs.

For what purpose?
What will that do for you?
What will that allow you to do?
What do you want from a....?
What are you looking for in a....?
How will you know when you have....?
What's important to you about?
What do you value most in a....?

D. Our Own Perception Of The World

The words that we all use during a conversation are not the experiences themselves. They are just the best verbal representation we can come up with. This is worth bearing in mind the next time that you have put a question to a prospect and are listening to his response. How precise is he?

The principal aim of your sales presentation is to elicit information to enable you to offer a deal that will be accepted by your prospect. If you don't get the right information your persuasive efforts will miss their mark and leave you without the sale. The questioning technique taught in this book will give you the linguistic technology to home in on the specific information necessary to close a deal. Have you ever been confident of winning an account only to be surprised to learn that it went to the competition? That is because your questioning wasn't precise enough to uncover the buyer's strategies, motivation and needs – or your understanding of the words he was using had a different meaning in his mind than it did in yours.

For example:

In the future customer's mind: I don't want to buy from this salesman, because the last time that I bought this sort of product the quality was poor. This led to the production line being stopped meaning thousands of pounds worth of product were written off. When I contacted the then sales rep he didn't want to know. From now on I'll be wary of an attractive looking price and have 'quality' and 'after sales service' as my top priorities.

Future customer: 'Good Morning, what have you got to offer me?'
Sales Rep: 'Good Morning, A great product range at prices that beat all of our competitors. How does that sound?'...
The Sales Rep continues, totally missing the mark.

The challenge to the salesman is to uncover the first paragraph from the sentence that he receives.

So the first step is to ask intelligent and precise questions with a clear outcome in mind (you are not there just to make friends).

Bear in mind that the value of a well chosen question is lost if you do not listen attentively to the response. In this context, remember that listening also means attention to tonality and careful observation of the speaker.

There are three types of homing-in or targeting question: barrier breakers, bridge builders and confusion clearers.

E. Barrier Breakers

Absolute barriers come in two main forms which I will refer to as 'brick walls' and 'sweeping statements', as further explained below.

Brick Walls

Examples of 'brick walls' are:

I can't give you the order.

I can't change suppliers at this time.
I won't consider using you again.

The targeting questions to deal with these must challenge assumptions about the past or habitual buying behaviour and introduce new options in the prospect's mind:

What would happen if you did?
How do you stop yourself from...?

Sweeping Statements

Examples of sweeping statements are:

I have never been satisfied buying insurance.
All salesmen in my experience tell lies.
Every purchase I make is through Bloggs & Co.
I always buy on the basis of lowest price.

When a future client makes such a statement, it is very rare for it to be true in the client's mind for all occasions. By getting them to show you the exception you can prise it open, offering choices to the client that were not there before.

Targeting Questions to deal with these would be along the following lines::

Never?
All?
Every?
Always?
Has there ever been a time when....?

Bear in mind a statement that the prospect makes will often provide choices as to what may be challenged. The real talent is deciding which question asked is most likely to lead the prospect to the desired outcome.

F. Bridge Builders

Sometimes customer resistance is expressed in language that can be turned to your advantage, enabling you to pick on a point of expression and build a 'bridge' to cross the divide the customer is creating, and progress the dialogue. Examples are set out below.

Vague Nouns And Verbs

Statement: 'I want a better deal?'
Targeting question: *'What deal exactly would you like?'*
Statement: 'He ripped me off.'
Targeting question: *'How exactly did he rip you off?'*

Nouns Made Out Of Verbs.

A verb is alive, dynamic, open to change. A noun is fixed, rigid, lifeless, unchangeable. We can therefore put life back in by changing the noun back to a verb. For example:

Statement: 'I have made my decision.'
Targeting question: *'How exactly did you decide?'*

Missing People

Sometimes customers will make statements indicating that a third party has an influence on the decision. For example:

Statement: 'We'll think about this and come back to you.'
Targeting question: *'That's great, may I just ask who "we" are exactly?'*

Missing Information

Statements:

> 'I am not convinced. '
> 'I am undecided. '

Targeting questions:

> **'About What?'**
> **'About Whom?'**

Missing Comparisons.

Customers may make use of comparatives or superlatives with no mention of who you are being compared with.

> Statement: 'Bloggs products are better. '
> Targeting question: **'Better, in what way?'**
> Statement: 'Bloggs's products are best.'
> Or, 'Your product is too expensive.'
> Targeting question: **'In comparison to what or whose?'**

G. Confusion Clearers

Sometimes the customer will make a statement which is confused, or makes unwarranted assumptions.

Tied Statements

This is where two statements are ostensibly linked but the link between them has not been established and needs challenging.

Statement: 'I cannot decide today because my Purchasing
Manager is out. '
Targeting question: *'How does his being out stop you from
making a decision?'*

Opinionated Statements

This is the case where opinions, values and judgements are given with
out any supporting evidence. The source of the value needs to be
recovered.

Statement: 'Sales Representatives will say anything to get the
order. '
Targeting question: *'I am curious to know, what leads you to
believe that?'*

Mind Readers

Sometimes customers will indicate they know another person's
thoughts on a matter.

Statement: 'My MD wouldn't like me to change suppliers. '
Targeting questions: *'How do you know that?'*
Or, *'What leads you to believe that?'*

Cause And Effect

Statement: 'Because of current policy I am restricted in my
options.'
Targeting question: *'How specifically does current policy restrict
you?'*

Presuppositions

Sometimes a customer will make a statement including an incorrect presumption, or presupposition.

> Statement: 'I cannot make a decision until I have your discount rates.'
>
> Targeting question: **'What leads you to believe I have discount rates?'**

Note that as well as challenging presuppositions in others, you too can use presuppositions or presumptions for your own purposes. They are persuasive because they make linguistic short cuts in the future client's mind. Consider the following:

Did you know that...?
Are you aware that...?
Perhaps you have already heard that...?
Have you ever noticed the fact that...?
Would it be fair to say that...?
Would you agree with me that...?
Would you agree with the experts that...?

Difficult not to answer 'yes' to questions beginning with these words. Bear in mind that you have not even heard the content yet and you are already agreeing. So will your future client. They are presuppositions because what follows is already established as fact.

This technique is even more powerful if you incorporate something the future client has already told you:

> 'Since you have already met the representatives from my competitors, would it be fair to say that if I can come up with a product that totally satisfies your needs at a competitive price you could make a decision today?'

The 'alternative close' also involves a presupposition:

'Would you prefer this model in red or blue?'

This presupposes that you are going to buy.

Consider the following questions. Can you identify the presuppositions?

How easily can you make a choice today?
Are you still interested in a new car?
When would you like to begin to consider the alternatives?
Have you allocated your budget yet?
How many of the beneficial points that you have learned today do you plan on sharing with your staff this week?
Have you noticed how well this car matches your personality?
What would it take for you to make a decision today?

Exercise

Think of three presuppositions that you could use in your sales presentation:

1. ....
....

2. ....
....

3. ....
....

Remember, the effect of a presupposition depends on the level of rapport. If you do not have rapport the question might not be answered at all. It is only necessary that the prospect thinks of an answer even at a subconscious level for it to have it's affect.

H. There Is Always An Easier Way!

Some students were having a charity race. The participants had to get to Aberdeen from Oxford without any money and without using public transport. For everybody who achieved it within 12 hours £200 was donated to charity, within 24 hours £100 and within the weekend £25.

The different approaches to this problem by various students were incredible. Out of 145 entrants only five completed the task winning the £200 for charity. Their approaches varied. One student chose to hitchhike. Nothing original in that – however, he was a mathematics student and he contacted the RAC and gained detailed information on traffic flows. Armed with this knowledge he did not hitch in the same way as he would have driven. Those who went as they would have driven it were delayed at points with little traffic flow and failed to meet the deadline. Another student contacted a car factory in Cowley and offered to deliver a car to Scotland free of charge. They were well pleased. At the end of the weekend the student's union had calls from all over Britain – one even from Wales. How did he get there? The losers had lots of good reasons why they were disadvantaged or unlucky. The winners didn't think of it as much of an achievement. It was easy for them.

Now, let us see how we can get to our objective by the shortest route, by looking at two examples.

Future client 'Your product is too expensive.'
Salesman: 'Compared to what?'
Future client: 'Well, compared to our present supplier, brand X.'
Salesman: 'How exactly does that product compare to mine?'
Future client: 'I don't know exactly.'
Salesman: 'That's interesting. What would you do if you were convinced that our product was of higher quality.'
Future client: 'I'd consider it, I guess – if you proved that it was better quality.'
Salesman: 'What exactly could I do that would satisfy you beyond doubt that my product is of better quality?'

Future client: 'Well, if we used them in our factory, under our working conditions and the defective rate was significantly improved.'

Salesman: 'What exactly would that be worth to you?'

We have steered the conversation from generalisations to specifics. Now we are in a position to offer our solutions that meet the client's true needs, not just the apparent needs – in this case a lower price.

There is always a question you can ask that will lead you to the business.

The second example is an ordering problem:

Future client: 'I have had a problem in the past when ordering new components.'

Salesman: 'A problem in ordering what specifically?'

Future client: 'Well, it's just that the quality has not always been what it could.'

Salesman: 'How exactly has the quality been lacking?'

Future client: 'You know, early failure of parts, defective units, that kind of thing.'

Salesman: 'Which parts in particular?'

Future client: 'Well now that you mention it, it seems to always be the control dials that are faulty.'

Salesman: 'What control dials' are you using?'

Future client: 'The Motorola RX400 series mainly.'

Salesman: 'On what applications do you use the RX400?'

Future client: 'On radios.'

Salesman: 'On all of the radios?'

Future client: 'No, not really on all.'

Salesman: 'On which ones then?'

Future client: 'On the class A and B radios.'

Salesman: 'Let me touch base. Your main problem at the moment is to do with the control knobs on the Class A and B radios. Otherwise there are no major areas for concern at the moment?'

Future client: 'Yes, that's right.'

Salesman: 'OK. What would it be worth to your company to have a reliable source of control knobs for these classes of radio?'

Future client: 'Well, I suppose if they were reliable we would have less stoppages, which is our hidden cost. However we have used other suppliers before and never had the reliability we wanted.'

Salesman: 'Has there ever been a time of smooth production flow using these components?'

Future client: 'Well, now that you mention it before our present supplier was taken over, quality was better. But we were paying higher prices then.'

Salesman: 'How does the previous higher price compare with the current additional price of stoppages?'

Future client: 'Mmm. I see your point.'

Salesman: 'OK. Let me tell you what I propose, and see what you think. My company's market research department has reported a lot of dissatisfaction from purchasers like yourself. The recession has made us all cost and price conscious in order to be competitive. In order to keep prices competitive, many companies have had to reduce their costs, which means that standards of quality have had to be compromised. The result is while some products appear cheaper in the short run, they can be considerably higher in the long run. Recognising this trend, our company's policy has been the opposite to our competitors. We have invested in R & D instead of cuts and employed rigorous quality control standards in our factories. We believe, looked at over the long run, our products are the best value for money on the market. Can I suggest that you try us out in order to see for yourself?'

Future client: 'Yes, OK.'

Salesman: 'What evidence would you need to know beyond reasonable doubt that our products were more suitable for your needs?'

Exercise

Respond to these statements with a targeting question.

1. The competition has a better product.

....

....

....

2. If I get an attractive offer, I'll probably take it.

....

....

....

3. I can't do that at the moment.

....

....

....

4. I can't make a decision over the phone.

....

....

....

5. I never buy anything before thinking it over.

....

....

....

6. All the salesmen I have met are pushy.

....

....

....

7. I am looking for something different.

....

....
....

Exercise

Write Your Own Empowering Versions Of These 'Self Ask' Questions.

1. How can I take total control of my sales results?
....
....
....

2. What is the most valuable question I can ask? (To yourself prior to a sales presentation)
....
....
....

3. What would I have to do in order to win your business? (During a tough presentation when you are coming up against resistance. Notice the hidden presupposition.)
....
....
....

4. How can I win this account?
....
....
....

5. What could I change in order to win your business?
....
....
....

6. What can I do today to excel?

....

....

....

7. How can I turn the situation to advantage?

....

....

....

With the knowledge of what you have learnt, what new closing questions can you think of that are relevant for your business?

....

....

....

....

....

....

As a final tip always pre-think your questions; for phone work, have them printed and in front of you for quick reference. For example, when trying to get through secretaries, 'Would you put me through to Mr Smith, please?' is stronger than 'Is Mr Smith available?'

6

Turning Objections Into Benefits
Through Verbal Aikido

A. Let Us Look At Objections In Your Business

Think of three objections that you regularly come up against in your business; write these in section A. In section B enter how you currently deal with the objection. Leave section C blank for the moment (we will be coming back to this at the end of the chapter).

1. A. ....
....
....

B. ....
....
....

C. ....
....
....

2. A. ....
....
....

   B. ....
....
....

   C. ....
....
....

3. A. ....
....
....

   B. ....
....
....

   C. ....
....
....

B. What Is Verbal Aikido, Why Is It Different?

Verbal Aikido is a method of objection handling that avoids head-on clashes and utilises the power of the objection in our response. This is done by gaining access to something that already exists. It gets the future client to look at something differently – not differently our way, but differently his way. That is why it is so powerful a technique. The most important thing to remember is that everything is relative; an event only has meaning to an individual in the context of their own experiences and assumptions. Change the context or the assumptions and you change the meaning.

For Example: What does heavy rain signify?

Bad news if you have the washing out.

Good news if you are a farmer suffering drought.
Bad news if you are having a garden party.
Good news if you are at sea, without water.
etc.

The meaning of any event depends on how you look at it. When you change how you look at it, the meaning can also change. When meaning changes, so can responses and behaviour. Therefore, developing the skill of applying Verbal Aikido to events or situations in the prospect's mind (that is, changing the way the prospect looks at the events or situations) will give you greater freedom and choices within the prospect's model of the world. This is because the 'event' or 'concern' itself has been totally respected – therefore so will the new way of looking at their objection.

Imagine that a future client says to you, 'Your price is too high.' Ever had that experience? We tend to add our meaning to that statement, which is often quite different from the meaning intended. It could mean any of the following, for example:

He believes he is not getting value for money.
He wants something for nothing.
He does not know what prices involve or include.
Thinks that he cannot afford it.
He can get the same service more cheaply.
Hasn't made comparisons.
He is out for a discount.
Benefits plus Service equals Price does not add up.
It is his job to say that.
He wants to know more.
He is testing you to see how you react.
First thing that came into his head.
He may have a fixed budget in mind.
His previous purchase was cheaper.
Bad experience of service.
Wants to hear why he should pay this price.
It is a total red herring.

It could mean any of the above and a whole lot more. So before we deal with an objection we must ascertain what exactly he means. Depending on what he means will determine the best response.

Verbal Aikido responses are therefore found by asking these questions:

> *'How can this objection/limitation/problem be turned to advantage?'*
> *'What is the useful value of this behaviour/fact?'*

It is not enough to satisfy the prospect on an objection; that is the limiting fact of traditional objection 'handling'. Our objective is to actually turn it into an advantage. Therefore objections should be received with relish as they will offer a short cut to the close. Your future client will be given more ways to look at problems, and the more ways you look at problems the more solutions there will be. The really adept lead the future client to these solutions rather than providing them. This way he answers his own objections in the way that is most meaningful and acceptable for him.

To save time I have classified thirteen techniques of Verbal Aikido. In different circumstances for different future clients, some will lead to a better outcome than others. It depends on the specific circumstances but they fall broadly into two categories. The first is where the context is changed and the second is where the interpretation of the meaning is changed.

Remember that the effect of the above will be stronger if you have developed a deep rapport. The responses can begin with the following to maintain rapport:

> 'I appreciate that, and....'
> 'I agree, and....'
> 'I respect that, and....'
> 'That's right, and....'

(Remember that disagreeing with matching body language will give stronger rapport than agreeing with mismatching body language.)

C. The Objection To Benefit Matrix.

On the next two pages are worked examples of the thirteen approaches to Verbal Aikido. The examples lists thirteen different responses to turn a first a pricing objection and then a no-change objection into a benefit. The actual choice of response will vary according to the context and the particular future client. Work through the examples for each heading, appreciating what is likely to happen in the future client's mind with each response. Consider where the conversation and his thoughts are being led. Then when you feel comfortable with the worked examples, go to the next page and put in the first objection you listed in section A at the beginning of this chapter. Complete the list of alternative responses. When you have finished this, do the same on the following pages for the other two objections you listed. You will soon find that you begin to appreciate exactly why this approach is so powerful.

D. The Salesman's Lucky Thirteen.

1. 'Your Prices Are Too High'

REDEFINE
Expense is relative..

POSITIVE INTENTION
You are looking then for best value for money

COUNTER EXAMPLE
Have you bought something expensive before and been satisfied.

PARALLEL STORY
I bought a cheap car, it broke down!

ONE VIEW OF THE WORLD
In comparison to what?

CHANGE THE TIME FRAME
Time will show the full story

APPLY TO SELF
With respect that is your belief

LEVEL UP
Aren't most things expensive these days?

LEVEL DOWN
What aspect of our service specifically.

ELICIT VALUES/CRITERIA
What exactly are you looking for?

SET A FURTHER OBJECTIVE
Using our service will aid your end objectives.

POSITIVE CONSEQUENCE
The quality of your products will improve.

NEGATIVE CONSEQUENCE
So you might miss an opportunity worth having.

2. 'It Is Difficult To Change Suppliers'

REDEFINE
It's not really difficult, it just requires thinking through.

POSITIVE INTENTION
You will presumably consider all the options carefully then.

COUNTER EXAMPLE
Has any successful decision you have made not been difficult in
    some way?

PARALLEL STORY
I have been finding it difficult to change my diet and lose weight....

ONE VIEW OF THE WORLD
That's just your perception; in reality you may not find it as difficult
    as you think.

CHANGE THE TIME FRAME
With hindsight haven't many previous changes turned out easier
than you thought.

APPLY TO SELF
Believing that makes it seem difficult.

LEVEL UP
Most worthwhile changes are difficult.

LEVEL DOWN
Only the first step is difficult.

ELICIT VALUES/CRITERIA
How have you got over this previously?

SET A FURTHER OBJECTIVE
It's difficult to get the best prices and service.

POSITIVE CONSEQUENCE
That ensures we will respect winning your business.

NEGATIVE CONSEQUENCE
Present suppliers can take your custom for granted.

3. *Your First Objection From Section A*

....

REDEFINE
....

POSITIVE INTENTION
....

COUNTER EXAMPLE
....

PARALLEL STORY
....

ONE VIEW OF THE WORLD

....

CHANGE THE TIME FRAME

....

APPLY TO SELF

....

LEVEL UP

....

LEVEL DOWN

....

ELICIT VALUES/CRITERIA

....

SET A FURTHER OBJECTIVE

....

POSITIVE CONSEQUENCE

....

NEGATIVE CONSEQUENCE

....

4. Your Second Objection From Section A

....

REDEFINE

....

POSITIVE INTENTION

....

COUNTER EXAMPLE

....

PARALLEL STORY

....

ONE VIEW OF THE WORLD

....

CHANGE THE TIME FRAME

....

APPLY TO SELF

....

LEVEL UP

....

LEVEL DOWN

....

ELICIT VALUES/CRITERIA

....

SET A FURTHER OBJECTIVE

....

POSITIVE CONSEQUENCE

....

NEGATIVE CONSEQUENCE

....

5. *Your Third Objection From Section A*

....

REDEFINE

....

POSITIVE INTENTION

....

COUNTER EXAMPLE
....

PARALLEL STORY
....

ONE VIEW OF THE WORLD
....

CHANGE THE TIME FRAME
....

APPLY TO SELF
....

LEVEL UP
....

LEVEL DOWN
....

ELICIT VALUES/CRITERIA
....

SET A FURTHER OBJECTIVE
....

POSITIVE CONSEQUENCE
....

NEGATIVE CONSEQUENCE
....

E. Benefits/Dangers Of Negatives

In your responses take care when using negatives in your language. Negatives exist in language but not in experience. For example, without adding further content what comes into your mind when you consider 'The sales rep is not on the phone'? Basically, it is difficult to think of something not happening; we usually have to think of it first in the positive in order to consider it. To illustrate consider what comes into your mind after reading the following:

Do not think of an elephant.
Now keep not thinking of that elephant.

Chances are you found it hard not to think of an elephant. The effect is even stronger if heard and not read.

Now consider these – which ones do you think you should use and which ones should you be careful to avoid:

'Do not think that you have to decide today.'
'Do not worry about the price for the moment.'
'It is not expensive.'
'I think you will agree it is not bad.'
'I don't want you to worry about delivery.'
'Do not drink and drive'.

You may like to consider the effect of the following:

'Do not walk on the grass.'
'Do not smoke.'
'No entry.'

F. The Effect Of Verb Tenses

Notice the difference between 'I will ring you in three months to see what you think of the products', and 'I will visit in three month; at that time we can look back at how the products have improved your general operations.'

In our brains we code time. As you might imagine, the future for most people is hazy and uncertain whereas the past is clear and concrete. When you use the future tense therefore the subconscious mind says 'maybe'. When you use the past tense it is accepted by the subconscious mind.

The way to adapt this for your business is by projecting yourself into the future looking back. How can you use this knowledge in your sales calls?...

G. The Power Of Parallel Story Telling

An analogy (or a metaphor) is a story implying a comparison. Communication through analogy can be a very elegant way of bypassing the conscious processes and influencing the unconscious mind directly. Metaphors are a powerful way of influencing. They can be attention-getting, by putting colour, sound and movement into your description. They can appeal to the emotions, by introducing emotive imagery or description. Stories are better recalled than bare facts, and at a deeper level. (A fuller understanding of why the effect of metaphors is so powerful can be obtained by a study of Ericksonian Language Patterns – see the bibliography).

The 'Third Party Quote Technique' is the most direct: for example, 'My previous call was to John Higgins the Purchasing Director of Science Systems. And he said "I have tried out your products and despite the fact that they are cheaper than the competition the quality has proved to be at least as good." What do you think of that?' Somebody else saying it has more influence than your saying, 'I know our prices are cheaper than the competition and that our quality is better.'

The quotes technique also has the advantage that if it goes wrong, the position is recoverable because the statement is attributed to a third party and not yourself. It is thus a good way to try out unsure ground to test the response before committing yourself. For example, 'I've just left John Higgins of Science Systems, who said to me that the potential of this product is so great you have got to be crazy not to at least try a sample order.' Less dangerous to try this by using the 'Third Party Quote Technique', isn't it?

Another method is to make a longer story introducing analogous characters, places, situations, decisions, etc., to the ones in the current situation; then leading to a solution in the story which the unconscious mind will automatically adapt for the present situation. Hence the term 'parallel story'. This is perhaps more easily explained by example.

Which of the following two narratives makes the point more strongly?

- 'In life it is best to make a plan and stick to it rigidly. Know clearly where you are going from the outset and not get diverted on the way. Studies have shown that people who adapt this policy tend to do better in their career than people who do not.'

- 'A friend of mine went into Victoria Station and approached the ticket booth with a fifty pound note in his hand. He said, "I would like to go somewhere really nice and attractive. I am not really sure where but I am very determined to arrive." The ticket clerk looked at my friend and said, "If you don't know exactly where you want to get to how do you expect us to get you there?"'

Design parallel stories that are tailored to fit the problem of your clients. Future clients will have unfulfilled desires because of limitations in their model of the world. You can create specific parallel stories that expand the range of the future client's world and guide him to fruitful outcomes.

To make a closing parallel story:

1. Examine the problem/objection.
2. Identify all nouns/processes.
3. Select content of story.
4. Create a noun/process in the story for each noun/process in the problem.
5. Design the story ending for a desired response.

It is not necessary to think on your feet; all you have to do is prepare up to five worked-out and rehearsed stories that will parallel and deal effectively with any objections that you are likely to come across in your sales visits.

You could also design stories that use one of the main 'languages' referred to already in this book using the phrases outlined earlier.

I was recently with a future client presenting my case for choosing me for their sales training programme. He said that he liked me immensely but found it hard to choose me as I was significantly more expensive than my competitors. I responded with the following parallel story.

A close friend of mine, Harry, wanted to buy a new car. He looked at more than half a dozen new models in their respective showrooms. He analysed their prices against various performance criteria. The more he probed, the more information there was to compare and the harder a decision became. He asked his MD for his opinion. 'In my experience I have found that the best strategy in the long run is to choose the company where the salesman in your opinion is the one with the maximum integrity, honesty, etc. Then when he makes a claim on a benefit you can believe it to be true. You usually get what you pay for and lower prices often mean lower quality somewhere. After-sales service is likely to be better and not based on empty promises. Only after you have had a new car for a year are you really in a position to judge what it was worth.' Harry then gave his order to the person that impressed him the most and he has not looked back on the decision.

My client was clearly influenced by considering Harry's experience and could think of similar examples from his own business experience. I now deliver regular training courses for the company and the client has said that I have made a significant contribution to their sales growth and increase in market share.

Expressing yourself by putting pictures into the client's mind is a very powerful way of communicating your message. It can also be done in sales letters – as in the following that I use with very successful result:

To: The Managing Director
ABC Company

Dear Sir

<u>Applying NLP To Selling</u>

I dreamt last night that I was a salesman who went back in time to the Roman Invasion, taking with me a warehouse full of Cruise missiles. I approached local leaders communicating the benefits and using all types of closes. It sounded too good to be true, which made them sceptical. They had extensive battle experience, believed that they knew everything and that I was trying to dress up old products in new packaging.

I then woke up and thought about the dilemma of the dream. NLP is new – it promises to transform, not just increase, performance. Nobody was going to be convinced of what Success Express could do for them just by being told about it. They had to see us in action.

We decided to run a subsidised half-day seminar for management on their premises, giving a thorough overview of what was on offer. Then they could decide from strength without making a major commitment. The seminar is run by two top trainers and costs just £349 inclusive of manuals etc. Any number can attend. On that seminar they would be taught specific new techniques that would transform sales performance.

If you have not experienced NLP, applied to a business context, prepare to change your beliefs on what can be achieved.

Please ring now to arrange a seminar.

Thank you for your attention.

Yours faithfully,

A. McMillan

H. The Power Of Visualising What You Want To Say

When we use metaphor or analogy in short phrases, it can be as powerful as a longer prepared story. If the customer's mind is helped to 'picture' what you are saying the effect will be several times more powerful. Try replacing the first of each pair of responses listed below with the second (i.e. replacing (a)with (b)). Reading through you will start to see (literally) why response b) is more influential. Learn a few by heart and get into the habit of using them – you will be startled at how persuasive and clear you become to your recipient.

a) I will try hard.
b) I will give it my best shot.

a) You cannot refuse this offer.
b) Don't look a gift horse in the mouth.

a) Try it and see.
b) The proof of the pudding is in the eating.

a) There must be some advantage.
b) Every cloud has a silver lining.

a) You should prepare for all eventualities.
b) To have more than one string to one's bow.

a) Working hard.
b) To be going full swing.

a) It is not difficult.
b) It's as easy as falling off a log.

a) No real gain.
b) To rob Peter to pay Paul.

a) Let us both work on it.
b) Two heads are better than one.

a) I think you are overemphasising the importance.
b) To make a mountain out of a molehill.

a) I know that it is true.
b) To stake one's life on it.

a) Uncommitted
b) To sit on the fence.

a) The same situation.
b) To be in the same boat.

a) I will listen.
b) I am all ears.

a) More than one benefit here.
b) To kill two birds with one stone.

a) To ignore what is going on.
b) To bury one's head in the sand.

a) Do not take the risk.
b) A closed mouth catches no flies.

a) Take action at the right time.
b) Strike while the iron is hot.

a) It's better not to procrastinate.
b) Never put off until tomorrow what you can do today.

a) To waste money.
b) To throw money down the drain.

a) It might seem better with closer inspection.
b) To judge a book by it's cover.

a) Take a chance and you will probably win.
b) Fortune favours the brave.

a) Do something about it.
b) Actions speak louder than words.

a) I agree.
b) Great minds think alike.

a) It could be the same again.
b) History repeats itself.

a) Let me be totally honest.
b) To put ones cards on the table.

a) The wrong way round.
b) To put the cart before the horse.

a) A certain success should not be put at risk.
b) A bird in the hand is worth two in the bush.

a) If you want to win you have got to take a risk.
b) Nothing ventured, nothing gained.

a) Best to be quick.
b) The early bird catches the worm.

a) Do not be impatient.
b) Rome was not built in a day.

a) To make contact.
b) To break the ice.

a) It will increase quickly.
b) To spread like wildfire.

a) To continue along the same path.
b) To keep the ball rolling.

a) Be careful.
b) To see how the land lies.

a) Be careful
b) All that glitters is not gold.

Think of situations where the following might be used to make your communication power more influential?

To kill the goose that lays the golden eggs.
There are plenty of fish in the sea.
A bird in the hand is worth two in a bush.
To let the cat out of the bag.
To see which way the wind blows.
To stand on one's own two feet.
A lot of water has passed under the bridge.
Look before you leap.
You can't have your cake and eat it.

I. Linking Cause With Effect

I see that you have read the brochure <u>and</u> are ready to decide.
<u>As</u> you read the brochure, you will notice how relevant the product is to your needs.
<u>While</u> you read the brochure, you will probably find things that are useful.
<u>When</u> you try out this new line, you will understand why I thought of you.

Notice how the underlined parts of the above sentences links two separate parts of the sentence. In none of the cases are the two parts necessarily linked in the implied way.

J. Tonal Marking

Many students have asked me about something they have heard called 'subliminal selling'. It was first used on television advertisements by inserting one frame saying 'You want a Fizzo soft drink now' into a normal advertisement. Now one frame takes a minute fraction of a second to run, and viewers would not be aware of seeing it at all. Nevertheless their brain received the image and the effect went directly to their unconscious mind. This practice, not surprisingly, was soon banned.

The term has reappeared more recently with the spread to the business world of NLP and Ericksonian Hypnosis. (Most of the adverts we watch on the TV today heavily rely on these techniques.) Subliminal selling in my experience tends to appeal to those who lack confidence and belief in themselves and their company's products. The idea of forcing someone to buy something against their is a last resort. Clearly it is a highly unethical practice. These techniques are, however, ethical when used by qualified and experienced hypnotherapists who need to stop their clients from hurting themselves. To have any effect the person using the techniques has to undergo lengthy training, but the principle can be shown in a simple example.

Consider how you might react if a salesman said the following to you:

> 'As you consider the alternative products you should be watchful that your decision to buy is only influenced by real value to you. My company's policy is to tell you about our products. Then leave you to make the right choice. Now, how does that sound?'

Now consider that the speaker 'tonally marks' certain words by emphasising them in some subtle way, slightly louder, slightly quicker or slower, whatever.

'As *you* consider the alternative products you *should* be watchful that your decision to *buy* is only influenced by real value to you. *My* company's policy is to tell you about our *products*. Then leave you to make the *right* choice. *Now*, how does that sound?"

Be on your guard against this sort of practice. When done by someone who is well versed in these techniques, they communicate their subliminal message directly to your unconscious mind. The unconscious mind picks it up and processes the idea, but does not communicate its activity to your conscious mind.

K. Presuppositions

We discussed the use of presuppositions in questions in Chapter 5. Now I would like you to consider how they are used in statements. In the following sentences the presupposition appears in brackets. Note that the statements are not intended as lies but present a more subtle way of transferring information than stating it directly.

They always prefer my style of presentation.
(There is a 'they'.)

I like salesmen that give me the 10% discount.
(There are already salesmen that give him 10% discount.)

If our major PLC customers didn't get next-day service they would have gone elsewhere.
(He has major PLC customers.)

If none of your competitors drop their prices, I'll give you the order.
(There are competitors.)

105

Several of the companies that have spoken to us left their brochures.
(Several companies have spoken to them.)

It was our new price guarantee policy that has maintained us as market leader.
(They are market leader.)

If you decide not to go ahead you can cancel up to a month.
(I don't expect that you want to cancel.)

What you'd like to order is probably from our new product listing.
(You'd like to order something.)

What your competitor can do to get my account is lower their prices.
(Your competitor can get my account.)

If you tell me your best price I'll decide now.
(There exists a 'best' price.)

If your price is as low as your competitor, we'll go ahead.
(Your competitor has a low price.)

I respect customers who choose our de luxe services.
(There exist such customers.)

If desperate salesmen don't get a deal they will drop price.
(Desperate salesmen exist.)

It was our fast service that persuaded your predecessor to order.
(Your predecessor ordered from us.)

I think this product line will continue to do well.
(It has done well.)

L. The Agreement Frame

'The Agreement Frame' is the result of extensive studies into top per-forming communicators. Tests have shown that when someone makes this technique a habit their results significantly increase. The tech-nique is simplicity itself:

Replace 'but' or 'however' with *'and'*. Thus:

'Yes, but...
'I see what you are saying, however...'
'I appreciate that, but...'
'I agree, but...'
'I agree with that, however...'
'That's right but...'

become:

'Yes, and...
'I see what you are saying, and...'
'I appreciate that, and....'
'I agree, and....'
'I agree that, and....'
'That's right and....'

Consider the following:

Client: 'Frankly, the service we had from your company last time we did business wasn't all that it could have been.'
Salesman 1: 'I appreciate that, but things have changed now and you need not worry anymore.'
Salesman 2: 'I appreciate that, and I will personally do whatever it takes to ensure that you receive the best possible service.'

M. Magic Selling Words:

The following fifteen words have been found to be the most frequently used by top performing sales professionals. What do you think might happen if you adopted them?

1. Discover.
2. Good
3. Money
4. Easy
5. Guaranteed
6. Health.
7. New
8. Proven
9. Your customer's name (in the same way they address you)
10. Results
11. Safe
12. Save
13. Own
14. Free
15. Best

Now, return to the exercise at the beginning of this chapter and complete section C with how you would *now* respond to the objections in A. You may be surprised at just how many alternatives you could apply to your business.

7

Selling The Way The Customer Makes Decisions

A. How Do Customers Analyse Information In Order To Make Decisions?

In this chapter we are going to take a look at how to size up a future client and tailor your presentation to their individual buying strategy.

Traditionally, sales professionals create empathy by finding out what their future customer is interested in and then talking about that. However if their interest is American football and you do not know anything about the subject you will be at a disadvantage. Establishing decision-making styles will help you to recognise *how* the person talks about American Football. If you can identify the types of information a person naturally responds to, and if you have the flexibility to offer the same kind of information, then you will be able to generate a feeling of understanding and enhance communication in a very powerful way regardless of subject matter. Like most of the techniques taught so far the real convincer of just how influential this simple technique can be is using it yourself.

Everybody sorts their experiences in terms of what is important for them. We reveal our methods for coming to decisions as we speak and after half a dozen or so sentences they rapidly become clear to the careful listener – what we talk about, what we leave out, what we complain about. You can find out someone's decision-making strategy by asking simple questions and listening. Having established them, you then incorporate them in your presentation. You will be talking their language; you will have rapport, attention and interest.

Any open-ended question will elicit someone's natural inclinations for analysing information. The really clever questions are those which also elicit their buying strategy, how they make decisions, and direct the client's mind towards owning what you are selling – for example, 'What exactly is it that you like about our products/services?'

B. The Main Ways Of Making Decisions

Now let us look at the most common styles of how people make decisions. As we discuss these they will start to fall into place as you identify people you know well making their decisions in this way.

Moving Towards vs. Moving Away From Preference

'Moving towards' people are motivated by promotion, pay rises, a bigger house, car, etc. They are moving towards those objectives. Anything you offer will stand a better chance of success if you show him how it can help him towards his objectives. Ask someone what motivates them and 'how' they answer will indicate whether they move towards or away from things.

'Moving away from' people want to move away from things – usually problems. For example, one customer of mine is not so much motivated by what he can get as by what he can avoid. He clearly wishes to feel secure and will move away from the threat of redundancy, losing his house, looking bad in front of colleagues, a demotion. I presented my case to him in these terms, making him feel confident that he was not exposed to risk and that it would make him more secure and thus more away from the things he wishes to be at a distance from.

Positive vs. Negative Preference

This way of making decisions is closely related to the ideas of motivation direction, towards and away from. Most things can be stated in the positive or the negative:

'How are you?' – Fine.	vs..	Not too bad.
I want a keen price.	vs..	I do not want a high price.
I am overweight.	vs..	I am not my ideal weight.
I want delivery this week	vs..	I do not want delivery after this week.
I want a good service	vs.	I do not want a bad service.

Whatever the topic some people will tend always to state things the positive way around, and some always the negative way. Most, of course, are somewhere in between, and for them this decision-making category does not apply.

Influence Direction Preference

When a buyer/customer/interviewer is influenced in making a decision about what he thinks about you, there are four possible sources of influence:

- *Yourself.* How do you sound and look to him. What are his first impressions about you? What people has he known in the past that you remind him of?

- *Others.* What would those that he knows and trust make of you? Another manager or colleague – or perhaps mentally asking himself, if xxxxx was here right now what opinion would they form?

- *Written and other material.* Your CV, sales brochures, reviews, articles, references etc.

- *A mixture of the above.* In practice one of the above patterns will usually stick clearly out in front. If this is the case, it means that the influence direction is not important for them and should be ignored. If, when weighing somebody up, you haven't decided in five minutes, you can safely ignore this category. This in itself is a valuable deletion.

Similarities vs. Differences Preference

'Similarities' deciders are constantly looking to compare any new information or communication with what they know. They match it up with something they are familiar with in order to judge it. When selling to someone like this you have to establish the favourable 'references' and make sure that you compare with these.

For example, on a recruitment assignment I was working on I noticed that the Financial Director (the client) constantly compared all the candidates to a previous employee he had once had. Clearly I was going to win a placement when I came up with a candidate with a similar background and personality. So I continued questioning about this previous employee. I found someone (who did not incidentally fit the formal specification at all) and gave him a thorough briefing before the interview. He was offered and accepted the job at interview. Needless to say the candidate was also a similarities decider and this is one of the reasons why they got along so well.

'Differences' people are easily spotted as they respond with the opposite or exception to what you are saying. Often such people are thought of as being deliberately difficult. However, they are just running their 'decision-making programmes' in the only way they know how. That is how they process and learn. Recognise this and respond in kind. You will have no doubt if someone is a difference decider – it is very easy to recognise.

For example, once while selling training seminars I recognised that my future client (prospect, if you want to start out courting failure) was a difference decider. So I changed my presentation and stressed the differences of my courses to alternatives. I was now speaking a language he understood easily – he was comfortable with what I was saying. Being on his frequency it was fairly straightforward from there to secure an order.

General vs. Specific Preference

General. The generalist likes to look at the big picture in order to get a clear impression before making a decision. Price is rarely a major influence on these people. Showing potential overall payback will be a far more effective selling strategy. Entrepreneurs such as Richard Branson tend to fall in this category.

Specific. These people want all the details and scrutinise the figures with a toothcomb. Your price will be looked at carefully in comparison to those of your competitors. This does not mean that specific deciders will choose the cheapest. In fact, they will analyse value for money of each alternative. Through a presentation they will constantly be asking you questions requiring very precise detail. Do your homework thoroughly and you will get the deal.

Past vs. Present vs. Future Preference

Past. These people when you listen to them are always referring back to past experiences. What happened in the past is a good guide for the future is a typical belief that they would have. 'We tried it that way last year in our Southampton factory and found that it did not work..' might be a typical type of statement that you come up against.

Remember your Verbal Aikido skills: try a question such as, 'Has there ever been a time that you have done it this way and it was successful?' With that question you are achieving two things. First, you are matching his 'past deciding' style. Secondly, you are challenging the implied assumption in his statement that because it did not work last year means that it will not work now (a complex equivalence in linguistic terms). The message here is obvious: if you have identified that someone makes decisions with reference to the past, tie your offer to his past successes. References and testimonials are very influential to these types of people as by indication they refer to the past. Past-oriented people invariably use the past tense of verbs, i.e. I thought, was, decided, etc

Present. 'What I want to know is what can you do for me *now*!' The word 'now' used repeatedly is a good indicator of a present-time person. Telling this person what you have done for others in the past or the effect of accepting your offer in six months will be a waste of breath. Present-time people are spotted quickly because they invariably use the present tense of verbs, i.e. I think, am, decide, etc.

Future. 'What will it do for me?' A 'future' person is always trying to get somewhere. Find out where that is and show him how you can help. Watch for frequent use of the future tense, i.e. I will, might, would, etc.: 'I can see where this will lead.' 'I will give you an order if you will shave 10% off price.' 'I will give it some thought.'

As you might have guessed, 'future people' tend also to be motivated more by moving towards 'good news' than distancing themselves from 'bad news'.

Short-Term vs. Long-Term Preference

Those who are orientated to the future (see above) are often easily divided into short- or long-term thinkers. In the recruitment industry this is a very valuable type of person. In considering a new candidate, does your client talk about what can be achieved in the next three months or three years? If three years, telling the changes that your candidate could achieve in the next three months won't get you far. Talk about long-term values, consistency, stability, seeing things through. A simple question such as 'What would you like the new candidate to achieve?' will soon supply you with the information you need. They will of course be giving you far more information than they realise.

Task vs. Relationship Orientated Preference

A very important category if you are looking for a job or trying to secure a brief as a recruiter. Ask: 'Tell me about the job itself?' Observe the way the employer or prospective client answers.

Other Decision Preferences

The above are the main categories of preference I have come across repeatedly. Very few people will not fit clearly into one of these. When you look for it the preferred way of making decisions will appear obvious. The method of making decisions is formed very early on in life and becomes part of the basic 'software' of how people make sense of the world around them. It will show up clearly in their general behaviour. Try to spot something in their language that keeps recurring. When you have this you have the key that will unlock their decision-making style. Other patterns that I have come across are:

> Money.
> Numbers.
> Places.
> People.

C. Developing Your Ability To Sell To Preferred Decision Styles

Once you have identified the decision-making method, the trick is to match your own approach and presentation to the that method. It will obviously be easy, if not automatic, to match the decision-making methods that are similar or identical to your own. The real skill in persuasion is communicating in a pattern which is not yours but that of the recipient of your communication. Often, particularly at first, it will feel unnatural by definition. Making this effort is what I call customer service. Many of my clients in the recruitment industry have told me that their staff seem to have great success with some clients while with others they don't seem to make any breakthroughs. Often the reason is that the successes are coming when they are talking to people with the same or similar ways of processing information as them. So I suggest before you start analysing what somebody else's decision-making methods are, find out what your own are. At the end of this chapter is an analysis sheet I have designed for this purpose. Ask your closest work and/or social colleagues to complete it for you.

Recognising and talking back to somebody in their preferred patterns is the quickest-to-learn and most practical sales technique that I have ever come across. It is also extremely powerful. I have personally observed individuals significantly increase their performance level by doing nothing more than concentrating on this technique.

The way to develop your skill at this technique is practice. It is best to practise in a controlled group with an experienced tutor. However, much learning can be gained by practising in your own group of at least three people and discussing the results. Put one person in 'the hot seat' and ask them any open-ended question. Ask them to tell you about their favourite sport, their holiday, whatever. Get them to talk for five minutes. Record what they say. If they falter, ask more open-ended questions to keep them talking. With reference to the assessment sheet at the end of this chapter, each of you assesses what you think are their preferred styles for all the categories. Then put a circle around the three that you think are the most critical. If there are any categories that you are unsure of, ask a question that will give you that information.

When you are ready, ask the person to leave the room. Exchange notes with each other until you agree the three most crucial decision-making methods. Then choose a 'matcher' and a 'mismatcher'. The job of these two people is to make a two-minute presentation to the person and try to sell them something. What you choose to sell is not important but it should be the same thing – for example, a house, a car, a holiday, a boat, an insurance policy. It need not be related to what the person spoke about. Now ask the person back into the room. The 'matcher' goes first and makes his sales presentation using the three key decision preferences. Then the 'mismatcher' makes his presentation.

To illustrate, say the agreed three key methods are, Past, Generalising and Differences. The 'matcher' sells his product with reference to the past, tried and tested, etc., with generalisations as to the benefits and applications while stressing the differences. The 'mismatcher' talks in the future about what will happen in highly specific details, stressing the similarities. Afterwards, sit down and ask the person from whom he would buy. When you are in the 'hot seat' it will amaze you how much more appealing the matcher's presentation is. This is a vital experience because you will appreciate just how powerful this simple technique is, and it will motivate you to become proficient at it, Your results in developing rapport and persuading will clearly increase.

Principal Preferences

Analysis Sheet

(Circle the decision-making method preferred)

1. MOVING TOWARDS / MOVING AWAY

2. POSITIVE / NEGATIVE

3. SELF / WRITTEN / OTHERS

4. SIMILARITIES / DIFFERENCES

5. GENERALISATIONS / SPECIFICS

6. PAST / PRESENT / FUTURE

7. SHORT-TERM / LONG-TERM

8. TASK / RELATIONSHIP

9. MONEY

10. NUMBERS

11. PLACES

12. PEOPLE

8

Objectives, Feedback And Flexibility: The Path To The Deal

A. The Importance Of Clarifying Objectives

Are you doing what you are doing because you really want to or because somebody else wants you to? How much are your objectives being influenced by others? How much time are you spending helping others reach their goals at the expense of yours?

Establishing clear objectives is one of the key things that identifies highly successful sales people. It brings with it commitment, direction and motivation. The more committed you are to something the easier it seems to become.

Have you ever watched a sales office, as a fly on the wall? There are two distinguishable groups of people: those who are permanently on the phone – if you ask them for five minutes of their time, they say no – and those who seem to be constantly searching through directories and old files – if you ask them if they can spare five minutes the answer is, yeah sure. The difference is usually that the former group are working towards clear objectives and are not prepared to be digressed. If that means doing telephone cold calling which they don't like, they have the attitude:'I'm going to get through it as quickly as possible in order to get to my objectives beyond.' In fact, as they go through their calls quickly their time is mainly spent on interested future customers and they find themselves enjoying it.

Setting clear objectives is simple to do and time well spent.

1. Write down in specific terms what you want to achieve. Keep everything in the positive. Think in terms of what you want, not what you don't want. Remember what we discussed earlier on the subconscious effects of using negatives.

2. Determine how you will know when you have got it – a new house, a new car, a promotion, the prize for top salesman, £100,000.

3. Test each goal by asking, 'Are you prepared to do whatever it reasonably takes to achieve this?

4. Establish what exactly you will have to do to achieve your goals.

5. Type out the plan, broken down into objectives for each quarter that lead to your final target. Think of each quarter's objectives as rungs on a ladder. Then stick it on the wall or somewhere prominent where you will see it every day.

Let us make a start at number 1: what is it that you want to achieve?

From now on forget past results. Decide, in detail, what you want to achieve. OK, so we are going to define precisely what we want and then develop a clear plan to get it. List everything you want – take as much time as you need. A new house, a sports car, lots of money, two luxury holidays per year, a board appointment, promotion, to sell most in your company, write a book, lose that extra stone of weight.... Be as detailed as you can – for example, what new house exactly, what car exactly, how much money? Do this now on the following page in pencil and change it until you are totally satisfied. When you have done that imagine you are in the future at the time that you have all those things. Looking back to now, see what it was that you had to do that led to those achievements. This will help you in developing a clear plan and knowing exactly what you have to do and also what you don't have to do. If you are doing something that is not supporting you towards your objectives, drop or change it. Looking back from a future point is important as, firstly, it is a final check that you are totally sure that it is what you want to achieve. Secondly, by putting your achievements in the past tense your brain codes them as reality, as opposed to possible future events.

B. My Objectives

What I want

1. ....
2. ....
3. ....
4. ....
5. ....
6. ....
7. ....
8. ....
9. ....
10. ....
11. ....
12. ....
13. ....
14. ....
15. ....

Now, divide your list in terms of what you want to achieve within 12 months (ring the number) and those over a longer period. When you have done that put both lists in order of priority.

C. The Action Plan

How I am going to get what I want

1. ....

2. ....

3. ....

4. ....

5. ....

6. ....

7. ....

8. ....

9. ....

10. ....

11. ....

12. ....

13. ....

14. ....

15. ....

The above is what I am going to achieve by ....

Signed ....Dated ....

Witnessed ....Dated ....

D. The Final Step

Make a copy of the previous two pages and stick them on the wall where you work. This will constantly remind you of what you are working towards and provide a challenge every time you do something which is not taking you towards your goals.

Professional selling is the art of dovetailing your objectives to those of your future customer (or career ambitions to those of your company). To do this you need to establish both your own and your target's objectives. Having established your own objectives, you help your customer to ascertain what *his* objectives really are; then you show him how to achieve them, in a way that is consistent with the realisation of your own objectives.

The sales process is in fact an objective-setting exercise:

- Setting objectives for yourself.
- Eliciting your future customer's objectives.
- Dovetailing the two together.

Now that you have a clearly laid-out plan, the next essential stage is to get going!

E. Assessing Individual Body Talk

There are so many different possible expressions, combinations and permutations in body talk that a full listing would read like a French-to-English dictionary (to someone who doesn't speak French). In the face alone, with its complex system of muscles, there are over 15,000 different facial expressions that are possible. The more prominent ones are fairly obvious, and are certainly worth knowing. But what I am interested in here is the more subtle ones that are peculiar to the individual and are far more numerous. Body language signs are different for different people. Therefore you have to calibrate for each individual. This is best done by matching and getting into their world.

The best way to develop your skill in understanding body language is not by studying books at all. Get a partner to stand to the left of you, and then say something that he agrees with and believes passionately. Then get him to stand to the right of you, and say something that is an outright lie. Observe every muscle in his face; what was different? Colour, colour change, a slight twitch somewhere before a lie, a flick of the brow, a slower speed, different volume? Repeat the drill until you are confident that you have calibrated his physiological unconscious responses. He would have to have the acting ability of Richard Burton to disguise his true feelings.

As you become more adept you can repeat the exercise using less extreme examples. For example, get your partner to make statements about foods they like and foods they don't like. After each practice session you will be surprised at just how much information you can read from their face. Always remember that face-to-face communication is 55% pure body language and a further 38% tone of voice.

F. The Importance Of Flexibility

Once you have realised how vital it is to listen and observe for feedback, you now have to use that information skilfully. You must be flexible to continually alter your response to reflect a developing and changing situation. As you gather information through a presentation you must change your approach to match the new situation. Knowledge is only power when it is acted upon. Or to put it another way:

> *'If you keep doing the same things, you will keep getting the same results.'*
> *Or, 'You trim your sails to the wind that blows.'*

First read the signs (observation and calibration) and then adjust your behaviour accordingly to home in on your target.

What exactly is it that makes flexible behaviour so hard? Perhaps it is the fear of failure, or that you are not confident that your calibrations and deductions of what your future customer is thinking are right. In this case

If what you are doing is not producing the results, try anything else.

If sales presentations were suits, some would perfectly fit the customer and some would not. Quite often sales people win some accounts and lose others without really knowing the reason for either. My aim in this chapter has been to show you the importance of flexibility, to put those lost sales into the winning camp. When analysing sales success most people, particularly the managers, concentrate on what you did and then what the potential client did as if they were two separate entities. I would like you to start thinking of successful sales presentations as when two people behave as one.

This approach is in direct contrast to the 'numbers game' mentality. While credible evidence can be produced to show that selling is a numbers game, it is a dangerous belief to adopt. It firstly puts you in the frame of mind to accept the situations where you lost. 'Well, you can't win them all' say the supporters of this belief. 'Why not?' is what I want to ask. After each situation where you did not get all that you wanted ask yourself two questions.

- 'What could I have done differently to get a better result?'
- 'What can I do, right now, to change the result?'

These questions will focus your mind on learning from your experience and concentrating on further action.

G. The Power Of Multiple Perspectives.

As already discussed, our personal perceptions filter memories of events by generalising, making distortions and deletions. We cannot not do this. Therefore you will find that if you get two people to meet and then ask them independently to write a one-page summary on what transpired you will have a surprise. Reading such reports it is hard to believe that the participants ever met. This phenomenon is the reason why many sales are lost – remember the sales rep who thought things were going his way and was surprised when no order appeared?

Our perceptions of the world are completely individual to us, and as such have large holes. The technique of 'viewing positions' allows us to get outside of our own models of what transpired and see it as if we were somebody else.

Imagine if you could take the two people in business you most admire with you on every visit to give you feedback afterwards. This information would considerably accelerate your learning, from each experience, wouldn't it? After all, making mistakes, as long as we recognise them, is how we learn. And learning is how we progress to excellence and peak performance.

A 'viewing position' is the point of view from which we see the 'world' at any particular time. Developing the skill of taking regular differing viewing positions is simple and requires no more than a vivid imagination.

There are three main viewing positions:

• First Position: the sales representative.
• Second Position: the future customer.
• Third Position: a fly on the wall, noticing the communication between you simultaneously.

Following each presentation, take fifteen minutes with a pen and paper in a place where you will not be disturbed. First, run through the presentation again in your mind from start to finish. Run it slowly, and listen and watch as much as possible. With the knowledge of how the meeting actually progressed it will probably make more sense to you than it did at the time.

From the first position (your own), write down any notes that come to mind. Ask yourself what would you would do differently if you could wind the clock back.

Now take second position, this time imagining that you were the customer, looking through his eyes. What do you see? What do you now feel about the presentation of the person who has come into your office? You will find that doing this exercise helps you tremendously in seeing why the customer reacted the way he did. Write some more notes. What would you now do differently with the totally new perspective of the customer's viewpoint?

Now, take the third position. In your mind, imagine that you are in a cinema watching a film of the presentation taken by a hidden camera. Imagine you have a remote control and you can freeze-frame, go slower, or replay selected sequences. What do you notice from this position?

In all three positions you will find it works better if you can allocate different locations. This will also help to identify which role you are playing if you run it through more than once or do it in a group.

Although it may seem a bit strange at first, in fifteen minutes or so this simple exercise will provide you with six months' worth of work experience – an accelerated learning path, I'm sure you will agree.

Psychologically what is happening is broadly as follows. Our unconscious mind records all information that we are seeing, feeling and hearing. However so that our conscious mind (left brain) is not overloaded it filters out most of the information concentrating on what seems the most important at the time. Consciously, therefore, we don't usually have access to all this information. When you use your imagination (which is a right brain activity) you access the unconscious and all the information that is there. What we are doing in this exercise is calling up the relevant files, viewing them at our leisure and then consciously drawing deductions and conclusions from them.

This exercise will take you from being clever to being wise. Its purpose is to provide you with the maximum amount of feedback possible. With that feedback you must be flexible to change your style accordingly in order to control the outcome of subsequent meetings.

H. Future Customer Analysis

Name: ....Position: ....
Company: ....
Address: ....
....
....
....Telephone: ....

Words: Repeated words   ....
                                    ....
                                    ....
              Repeated phrases   ....
                                    ....
                                    ....
              Favourite metaphor ....
                                    ....
                                    ....

Tonality: Volume: Quiet/Loud
                Pitch: Low/High
                Tone :   Soft/Harsh
                Speed: Slow/Fast
                Spaces: Short/Long

Language:

Pictures	*Feelings*	*Logic*	*Sounds*	*Smell/Taste*
See	Touch	Think	Heard	Smelt
Show	Warm	Know	Said	Taste
Focus	Pressure	Change	Listen	Sweet
....	....	....	....	....
....	....	....	....	....
....	....	....	....	....
....	....	....	....	....
....	....	....	....	....
....	....	....	....	....

Decision-Making Style: Moving towards/Moving away
Positive/Negative
Self/Written/Others
Similarities/Differences
Generalisations/Specifics
Past/Present/Future
Short-term/Long-term
Task/Relationships
Money
Numbers
Places
People

Result Of Call: ....
....
....
....

Next Contact/Objective: ....
....
....
....

9

Peak Performance Selling

A. The Success Index

Do the following attitudes and beliefs apply to you?

Yes/No

..............1. My confidence is unshakeable.

..............2. I am committed to constant and never-ending improvement.

..............3. I am resourceful and have the ability to do whatever it takes to succeed.

..............4. I see problems as challenges and react to them positively.

..............5. I have tremendous confidence in my talents and abilities.

..............6. I control my results.

..............7. I am committed to excellence.

..............8. Whatever my results are, I can improve them.

..............9. I am a 'do it now' person and manage my time well.

............10. I am eager to get into action as I wake up each day.

............11. I know exactly what I want to achieve.

............12. I learn by my mistakes. I look at failure as feedback for improvement.

............13. I, not external events, control my emotional state.

............14. I eat and drink healthily.

............15. I exercise regularly and sleep well.

...........16. I nearly always have an abundance of energy.

...........17. I believe that whatever results somebody else can get I can get.

...........18. I love cold calling and look forward to telling new people about my company.

...........19. I set daily outcomes.

...........20. I respect my colleagues and learn from them.

...........21. When I meet someone, I make my impression of them by how they come across (dress, body language, voice tone), rather than the specific things they say.

...........22. I expect to win the business when I visit a client.

...........23. I am constantly asking myself, 'what can I do to be a little better?'

...........24. I know how to use my physiology to control my state.

...........25. I vary my approach to each client.

...........26. If what I am doing is not getting the desired result, I experiment and try alternatives.

...........27. I know that my confidence and belief in my personal service is so strong it is contagious and itself convinces clients to use us.

...........28. Fear of rejection is a problem other people have.

...........29. Any resource a competitor has is nothing compared to my creativity, ability, enthusiasm and skill.

...........30. I am very happy when a colleague makes a sale, and welcome the added pressure to get going.

...........31. When I make a client presentation I feel that I represent the whole team and I don't want to let them down.

...........32. If I make ten unsuccessful cold calls in a row it will not affect my confidence for call eleven.

...........33. I rarely start sentences with 'I can't....'

...........34. I know how to use questions to direct my own mental focus.

...........35. I am an outstanding sales person.

...........36. Belief in success is essential, techniques only help.

...........37. I can maintain enthusiasm and drive after a setback.

...........38. I am a really good listener and miss little.

...........39. I am confident that I can develop rapport with anybody.

...........40. If a potential client said that our competitors were offering a lower price, it wouldn't make me drop mine.

...........41. If I don't get it right at first, I will keep trying.

...........42. We are much better than our competitors.

...........43. There is no such thing as a difficult client, only an inflexible sales person.

...........44. Whatever obstacle I come up against there is always a way through, I just have to find it.

...........45. I visualise a successful outcome before every sales call/visit.

...........46. I know thirty benefits for a client using our company.

...........47. I think of our competitors as coaches.

...........48. Whatever happens there is always good news in it somewhere.

...........49. Our main competitors will never be as good as we are.

...........50. I can tell what sort of a mood someone is in just by the way they answer the telephone.

Calculate your percentage of 'yes' responses. This represents your efficiency in using your current abilities. It also highlights the areas that need attention. A score of 70% means that your performance can be improved by 30% by improving confidence and beliefs alone!

If you got a 100% ask a colleague to complete it again for you!

If you scored less than 10% have you considered becoming an actuary?

Now highlight each 'no' answer and write it on a separate piece of paper. Write in the following question: 'What can I do to change this to yes?'

B. Getting Into Our Peak Performance State.

What sort of month have you had?

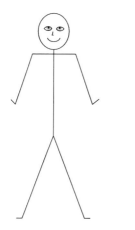 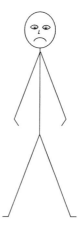

GREAT	**OH DEAR**
Smiling	Frowning
Head up	Head down
Shoulders up	Shoulders rounded
Firm stride	Slow walk
Talks Fast	Drawls
Positive words	Negative words
Excited	Depressed
Enthusiasm	Boredom
Looking up	Looking down

Our first communication is to ourselves.

C. The Importance Of State Of Mind

Richard, the Sales Manager for his advertising company, was on his way to a presentation with a potentially major account. His Managing Director called him on his mobile telephone: 'Hi Richard, Mark here. Great news, the company you visited yesterday are moving their entire account to us. That will make them our largest customer. Well done – incredible – we'll open some champagne on your return.'

How well do you think Richard will do at his imminent presentation?

Ten minutes later, while parking, Richard's telephone rings again. 'Richard, bad news, I'm afraid. Their FD has just rung and said that as we are relatively small, we are vulnerable and they cannot risk placing their entire account with us. Could you call in on them before returning and see if you can do anything?'

Now how well do you think Richard will do at his imminent presentation?

Same person, same experience, same knowledge, same abilities, etc., but his performance level can be changed in an instant. Lack of control of 'emotional state' loses more sales than lack of technique, experience or ability. Let us assume that Richard is an outstandingly consistent sales performer. He controls his 'peak performance state' as follows: before every customer visit he visualises his best ever presentation; he sees, hears, and feels it vividly as though it was happening now. This concentration clears out all other thoughts and gets him into a dynamic state for the presentation. All his resources are focused on the job in hand. He then walks in and gets the business.

Successful people, then, are those that are able to gain consistent access to their most resourceful states. When we create the appropriate 'state of mind', we create the greatest possible chance for using all our faculties effectively. Your behaviour is created by your state which in turn is determined by your physiology, which can be changed in minutes.

You can completely control your 'state of mind' and thus performance level by ensuring your whole physiology (body language) is vibrant, dynamic, motivated and positive. You can control your physiology by being healthy, which will create vitality, energy and enthusiasm. Health in turn is created by a balanced combination of exercise and a nutritious diet. It is a circle that can be used to support you. Be careful though – if the circle is overheated stress can sneak in, which can equally work around the circle destroying all the good work.

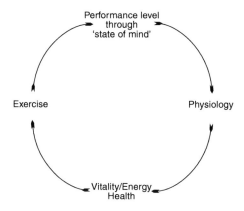

Figure 2. The Circle of Success

So at what point do you start on the 'circle of success'? Imagine you have to go for an interview or presentation today; how do you feel about it? The first thoughts and images that go through your mind as you imagine this should indicate your current state of mind, and from this you can determine your own start point on the circle.

Research has shown that nearly all highly successful people in business, politics, etc., have vivid imaginations. They see it, feel it, hear it, thoroughly experience it in their mind before they actually do it. They begin with an exact knowledge of what they intend to achieve before they actually do it. When they get into the real situation it does not scare them, because there is no unknown. They are confident; and through that confidence and mental preparation they are able to influence the way events turn out, and steer the events along their own preconceived routes. There's something rather amazing about what happens when you get a clear internal representation of what you want. It programmes your mind and body to achieve that goal.

You need to visualise a success in order to programme yourself to achieve it. Conversely, if you visualise failure you programme yourself to achieve it. Think now about going to visit the hardest, most unpleasant person in the world in the next five minutes to sell him something. What images immediately pop into your mind? If they are images of failure change them to images of success. Run through some images in your mind of everything going well. Notice how you have already changed the way that you think about the meeting.

Two salesmen walk into the Sales Director's office to report, following his return from holiday. He knows through body language alone as they walk through the door how things are, without asking the question. *If he can pick this up, so will customers.*

Suggestion: park away from clients when visiting and have a ten-minute brisk walk to their office. Remain standing in reception. Constantly check the relationship between your state, internal thoughts, physiology and results.

D. Peak Health

The mind and body are two parts of the same system. They work in unison and have a direct effect on each other. Neither of them can operate independently. The mind works at its best when the body is in a healthy, positive state. Top-performing sales people keep very fit! They exercise regularly, eat nutritious foods and avoid late nights. That makes them strong and resourceful and helps them to feel good and positive about themselves. And when we feel all these things we will attempt things that we would not normally attempt – and succeed at them.

Keeping healthy habits is an excellent start and an essential foundation for a successful state of mind. With this foundation in place, we can move on more effectively to the exercise of visualising successful outcomes (see previous section).Visualising confidence, success and peak performance will be made far easier the fitter, stronger and healthier you feel. This is what Olympic athletes do before the race. They run a movie in their minds of themselves winning their event – imagining victory, or perhaps recalling a recent event in which they excelled. They combine fitness and visualisation techniques to work towards a positive outcome.

Throughout the working day things happen and we react to them, changing our mental 'state' as we do so. The trick is to provide your own stimuli (run a movie in your mind of your greatest achievement) and thus control your emotional 'state'. I have noticed time and time again in sales that the real stars are the ones who can think positive and bounce back, even after a succession of rejections or setbacks – often even more determined than before. You now know how they do it. Most people, on the other hand, slow down and question their ability and skill, which in turn erodes their confidence. Hence the vicious 'circle'. They then lose the next deal.

As the body and the mind are totally related, anything less than peak fitness can only damage your results?

Answer the following questions:

What can I change to eat more healthily?

....

....

What can I change to drink more healthily?

....

....

What can I change to get more from exercise?

....

....

What will be the effect of the above changes on my performance?

....

....

What you eat, drink and think
determines your results.

E. The Highs And Lows

* What was your worst experience ever in selling?

....

....

* What was your most successful sales experience?

....

....

* What is the difference in how you 'code' these memories?

....

....

1) *How did you think when you succeeded?*

What did you see?

....

....

What did you feel?

....

....

What did you hear?

....

....

2) *How did you think when you failed?*

What did you see?

....

....

What did you feel?

....

....

What did you hear?

....

....

3) *What is the key difference between success and failure?*

What did you see differently between 1 and 2?

....

....

What did you feel differently between 1 and 2?

....

....

What did you hear differently between 1 and 2?

....

....

4) *What happens when you think about your failures in the same way that you think about your successes? How does it affect the feelings? What learning does this offer you?*

....

....

Most people find that they code 'success' and 'failure' in a completely different way. If you think in 'success' mode, this will help you to establish the expectation of success in your mind; your brain will then automatically adjust your behaviours to keep you on target to your new expectation. The answers to the above questions will provide your success keys when you think about a sales presentation coming up; force yourself to see, hear and feel it according to your personal success keys. This will ensure that you are in your most resourceful state.

F. The Success Cycle

Describe in detail your four greatest successes over the last year:

    (a) Describe what happened.
    (b) How you excelled.
    (c) What it felt like.
    (d) The positive things you told yourself and heard from others.
    (e) How things looked to you at this time.

1. (a) ....
   (b) ....
   (c) ....
   (d) ....
   (e) ....

2. (a) ....
   (b) ....
   (c) ....
   (d) ....
   (e) ....

3. (a) ....
   (b) ....
   (c) ....
   (d) ....
   (e) ....

4. (a) ....
   (b) ....
   (c) ....
   (d) ....
   (e) ....

Read through these success records daily to uplift your confidence

When our confidence goes up, it inspires us to take action. The more action we take, the greater are our results. Greater results create greater beliefs in our abilities, skills, potential, etc. The more empowering our beliefs, our confidence will be raised. This cycle can be triggered off from any start point.

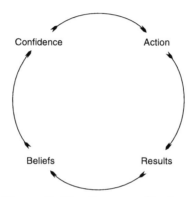

Figure 3. The Success Cycle

The converse is also true. After a bad result, a rejection or setback, our beliefs as to our abilities tend to be challenged. We ask ourselves negative questions like, 'Why does it always happen to me? Why can't I get it right?' These questions get answers which erode our supporting beliefs, replacing them with holding-back beliefs. For example: 'However hard I try I can never break the £10,000 of sales a month barrier; it just isn't possible for me.' Down goes the confidence. Due to low confidence we feel less inclined and motivated to take action. And so it goes on if we let it. Eventually something happens to reverse the process.

The average sales person is constantly having 'good runs' and 'bad runs'. The star performer has learnt how to maintain his personal success cycle. As soon as he senses something slowing down he notices corrects it and maintains his peak performance state. The first thing then is to notice the point of change from a good towards a bad run. The second thing is to increase any of the four critical parts of the success cycle. Some top performers just 'get their head down' and take non-stop action. Some use visualisation or a physiological change to get their confidence up. Going for a brisk walk or a tough work-out in a gym can be enough. Some read through their success and reaffirm their supporting beliefs. Most, however, wait for a lucky result to pick them up. This is the worst one to pick because results depend upon action being taken first, and while they are waiting confidence and belief diminish.

Referring to your four great successes, at what point did your Success Cycle start?

1. ....
2. ....
3. ....
4. ....

G. How You Can Create Unstoppable Self-Confidence

A confident state leads to target-busting results.

'Great State' = 'Great Results'

So how can we develop an unstoppable confidence?

Answer 1: Change your physiology radically.

- Go for a run or brisk walk.
- Take a break.
- Do some exercise
- Stand tall, breathe deeply, smile and look up.
- Tell a joke and enjoy a good laugh.

Answer 2: Control your mental focus.

- Expect the best to happen.

  What are you picturing, hearing, feeling in your mind? How do you do that differently for a resourceful or a depressed state? What are the 'keys' that will make your state instantly resourceful?

- Direct your mind to success with the right questions.

  'How can I turn this to advantage?'
  'What's the best way to achieve my objective?'

  'What opportunities are there here?'

The questions we ask ourselves have a direct influence on our state of mind. The answers are our evaluations. If we ask, 'Why does it always go wrong for me?' we will find an answer: 'Because I am no good, I just can't do it.' This evaluation will depress us. Our state of mind is a result of the questions we ask.

My favourite way of getting into a resourceful state is a brisk walk around the local area while concentrating on questions that direct me to what I wish to achieve.

When you are in your failure state what are the questions you ask yourself?

....
....
....

When you are in your success state what are the questions you ask yourself (and what are the answers)?

....
....
....

Ask other people why they are brilliant at something. Notice how this clearly uplifts their state of mind. All I am asking you to do is ask yourself the same questions regularly.

H. The Keys To Your Performance Level

I would now like you to do the following exercise, which will establish how you personally prepare yourself for success and failure. This exercise is best done in twos in a quiet place where you will not be disturbed and which supports concentration. Take turns asking each other the following questions. First you must elicit the desired state and not just interrogate them on it.

1. Tell them to think of a time (closing their eyes if helps) when they were incredibly successful. Tell them to imagine they are there now, enjoying that incredible success.... Continue talking them into this 'success state' until their facial expression indicates to you that they are there and not just saying it. Saying I have got a 'successful state' with a depressed look on the face is not convincing.

2. Now ask them to describe their internal experience in their own words. Ask them to describe what they see, hear and feel. Record this information on the form set out below.

3. Repeat steps 1 and 2 for their 'failure state'.

4. Ascertain what the critical differences are between the two experiences. Do this by your own judgement and reference to your notes and confirm by asking them.

5. Now take the 'failure' and get them to think about it in the same way as they do for a success. For example, let us say for a success they visualise colourful panoramic pictures, with loud voices of people telling them pleasant things. For a failure they visualise tiny black and white pictures with people murmuring behind their back about how incompetent they are. In this case, you say: 'Right with the failure in mind imagine you have a TV remote controller. I want you now to turn the colour up until the picture is quite attractive. Now I would like you to enlarge the picture until it is

all around you. Then change those voices to pleasant things and turn up the volume.'

6. Now ask them how they react to the 'failure' – how does it seem to them now? When you can clearly see that their physiology (body language) is the same as it was for their 'successful state' you have got their success key. This key is immensely valuable. They now know how to access their peak performance state at will, whatever the setback.

	Success	Failure
PICTURES		
Through own eyes or like watching a movie	....	....
Location	....	....
Distance	....	....
Brightness	....	....
Colour	....	....
Size	....	....
Clarity	....	....
Movement	....	....
Speed	....	....
Depth	....	....
Duration	....	....
Frame/Panorama	....	....
SOUNDS		
Inside/Outside	....	....
Location	....	....
Distance	....	....
Clarity	....	....
Speed	....	....
Continuous	....	....
Volume	....	....
Tone	....	....

Words/Sounds	....	....
Whose Voice	....	....
Mono/Stereo	....	....
Duration	....	....

FEELINGS		
Location	....	....
Extent	....	....
Shape	....	....
Pressure	....	....
Temperature	....	....
Movement	....	....
Duration	....	....
Frequency	....	....
Intensity	....	....
Texture	....	....

I. Turning The Keys

Now we know our keys, how can we use them to open the door to success?

1. Correct 'low' states immediately.

When you notice that you are 'low', correct it,

- Start thinking about the 'problem' with your success keys.
- See success, hear success and feel success.
- Adopt your physiology for success – stance, posture, breathing, facial expression, movement.
- Ask results-orientated questions.

2. Prepare For Action.

How do we sales people feel before a cold-calling session or perhaps a client visit. We sometimes have a problem with cold calling not because of lack of technique but how we 'set ourselves up' before calling. We picture aggressive prospects with loud voices telling us not to bother them. This belief in failure is transmitted through voice tone. Then, guess what? We fail. Then – guess what? – we tell ourselves: 'See I knew it was going to be difficult.' (Recognise the cycle?)

3. Take Action

J. Motivation - Avoiding Bad News, Seeking Good News

Are you motivated by avoiding bad news or seeking good news? In other words, is your motivation style based upon moving away from threats or towards rewards – moving away from the stick or towards the carrot? Most people are somewhere between the two and it is important to have some idea where, as this will determine where the emphasis should be for you when motivating yourself.

For example, let us say that you want to make fifty telephone canvass calls a day. However, somewhere along the way your motivation wanes and you never consistently perform the task as well as you would like. Typically nine out of ten calls don't produce a result. Therefore being rejected nine times (bad news) outweighs being accepted once (good news). To avoid bad news you therefore avoid cold calling.

How can you allocate more bad news to not doing the calls and good news to doing them? The answer is to allocate as much 'bad news' as possible to not doing them – and as much 'good news' as possible to doing them.

Bad News If You Don't Do The Calls

1. No future clients.
2. Less opportunity to earn commission.
3. Miss opportunities that were just waiting for the picking.
4. Beaten by competition.
5. Get fired.
6. Colleagues get the business and show you up.
7. Constant nagging pressure and guilt from not doing it.
8. Limited client base.
9. Declining size of client base
10. Less interesting work to do.

Good News If You Do The Calls

1. More commission.
2. Plenty of potential customers.
3. Breakthrough sales to a new level.
4. Feedback information on market conditions.
5. Satisfaction of success.
6. Money (list all the things that you want money for).
7. New car.
8. Every ten calls a result thus each call is 10% success.
9. Leads to promotion.10.Sooner done sooner can move on to more interesting things.

Compile your own lists, and when you have completed them as thoroughly as you can, read them and think about them before every canvassing session.

K. Morning Focus

Start the day as you mean to go on. Every morning ask yourself five questions that will get you into a resourceful state, focusing on achievement for the day. When you have decided on your five questions stick them on a wall so that you see them before you leave home in the morning.

Answer these questions every morning. Put them in a prominent place, where you will see them soon after waking up. They will immediately get your mind focused towards your objectives and provide you with a positive orientation.

1. What do I wish to achieve today?
    ....
    ....

2. Who would be really worth calling?
    ....
    ....

3. What could I do today that is different and useful?
    ....
    ....

4. What would make me happy if I achieved it today? What can I do to achieve it?
    ....
    ....

5. What would I have done differently yesterday if I had the chance?
    ....
    ....

What are the three most powerful questions that you can ask yourself in order to access your most resourceful state?

1. ....
    ....
    ....

2. ....
....
....

3. ....
....
....

L. Linking Your 'Peak Performance State'

When you geared up for in your peak performance state, wouldn't it be nice to be able to access it just by having a key that immediately opens it up? Well, if we think about it there are various naturally occurring 'links'. For example, when I listen to an old Beatles hit, it immediately takes me back to my teenage days to where I was living, what I was doing, the people around me at that time. It is a very nostalgic experience. In fact, for me – and for most people, I suspect – hearing any pop music hit, particularly if I really liked the group, takes me back to the experiences that I was having when it was in the hit parade. Do you have a piece of favourite music that takes you to a time when you were unstoppable? Other memories can also can affect my 'state' immediately – usually something involving high emotional content whether it be good or bad news.

Now the question is if these strong links occur naturally how can we harness that power to enable us to access our most resourceful, peak performance states when we need them? When we are naturally in our peak performance state – I mean really feeling good – we should introduce a stimulus at the height of the feeling – clench a fist, shout, 'Yes, Yes, Yes', play our favourite music... whatever. In fact, I have found that for most people certain music will already have strong emotions for them and uplift their state – for example, Land Of Hope And Glory, Chariots Of Fire, Theme To Rocky, Simply The Best, or the theme to 'The Dambusters'

Of course, as well as controlling your own emotional states, you will also want to elicit the 'state' of the recipient of your communication. For example, if you want a future client in a buying state, ask him about a time when he bought the type of product you are selling and ask him as much as possible about it. While you are gaining information about how he buys and what is important for him, he is reliving a successful purchase and cannot help but access his 'buying state'.

M. The Points Award Self-Motivation Scheme (PAS)

What is PAS?

PAS is an incentive programme designed to motivate people both on an individual and a team basis. It also allows you to monitor and review your own performance and have a useful yardstick from which to improve – the basic theme is, 'Never try to be better than someone else; be better than yourself'. PAS gives you the feedback that indicates where you can improve and what you have to do to prove that you have. Although you will want to know what other people are achieving, the important thing to remember is to constantly improve on your own performance.

Traditionally, building a reputation and a database of customers takes time. Often, when a client places an order it follows a period of selling activity over a number of weeks. Therefore, good work in one particular week will not necessarily be reflected in that week's performance figures. This can easily lead to declining confidence and motivation. The PAS gives you the opportunity of being rewarded now for the good work that you do (by knowing that you are progressing), and recognises the 'goodwill' value of every contact made. Over a period of time you will accumulate statistical information such as the average number of calls per deal done. This means that every call you make has a clear value. Your task then is not only to make more calls but to make the same number of calls more effective. You can start to look at this by analysing the approach of the sales person with the highest 'hit' rate and learn from their example.

How Does The Scheme Work?

The PAS scheme focuses on ten different areas of success in a marketing call from which you award yourself points. It is as simple as that. Week to week you coach yourself to ever-increasing performance. You will also find that you manage your time better.

Each day there will be a simple record form to complete as you go, which can also be used to remind you of call-backs, etc. At the end of each week you study your performance and set your own achievement targets for the following week which should be at least a 10% improvement.

Every monday morning you can review your PAS forms to discuss results and what can be done to improve.

PAS Daily Activity Sheet

Contact Co	Outcome	Points	Contact Co	Outcome	Points

One point awarded for each of the following:

1. Your company name plugged.
2. Relevant contact name(s) established.
3. Rapport established with relevant contact.
4. Favourable impression left.
5. Information on potential business.
6. Information on the company itself.
7. Objection overcome.
8. Client visit secured.
9. An order.
10. A sale (1 point per £100)

10

Empowering Beliefs: The Foundation For Success

A. What Are Beliefs?

Here are some different ways I define beliefs. Take a few minutes considering the meaning and significance of each to selling.

- A belief is not about reality, but it becomes reality for you.
- Beliefs are self-fulfilling.
- Belief systems are software for the mind.
- Whether you believe you can or cannot, you are right.
- A belief is a feeling of certainty.

A belief is an inner view or conviction which transcends reason and may not easily be changed by information alone, however contrary to the belief itself. The placebo effect in medicine is due entirely to the creation of a belief which belies the facts, and has important implications for professional selling.

The thing to realise about beliefs is that your actual behaviour will automatically adapt to meet them. In a conflict between a behaviour and a belief, the belief will usually win. Because of this, beliefs have a powerful self-fulfilling effect.

Within the sales context, there are three particularly important types of belief:

1. A generalisation about a limit.
   '£10,000 per month is the highest achievable sales performance'.
   'Four sales visits a day is the maximum possible.'

2. A generalisation about the cause of something.
   'Being over fifty stops me getting a good job'.
   'High quality training leads to high quality results'.

3. A generalisation about the meaning.
   'Average results means that I am average'.
   'Not having a degree means that my potential is limited'.

B. Why Are Beliefs Important?

Beliefs are important because when you change a belief your behaviours will change in order to live up to them. Behaviour is a function of the values, beliefs, needs and habits a person has. If you understand a person's values, beliefs, needs and habits you will start seeing patterns. When you understand the patterns you are in the inner workings of their behavioural impulse. Beliefs are a fundamental part of this process, and have a direct effect on an individual's behaviours.

We often create our beliefs with insufficient information, as our mind automatically fills in the gaps. Once accepted, our beliefs become unquestioned commands to our nervous system, and they have the power to expand or destroy the possibilities of our present and future. Beliefs can be supportive in their effects or hold you back. Limiting beliefs usually have their root in strong negative experiences, often a single one in which the belief was formed. It is not the events themselves of our experiences that shape us, but our beliefs as to what those events mean.

A manager I know recruited a new sales representative called John who, while excellent in the field, believed that he could not sell on the telephone. He would not even pick up the handset unless under close supervision.

The manager tried to convince John that he was actually quite good, and that in fact if he could sell face to face, selling on the telephone was easy. They had many arguments back and forth. Some past experience must have had a very profound effect on John to convince him that he was no good on the phone. Finally, the manager had an idea and said, 'Do all prospective customers tell lies about how they were influenced by a cold call from a salesman?' John thought about it and said, 'No, occasionally some might when it is in their interest to do so, but certainly not all.' So the manager said, 'OK let us try an experiment. I will ring the twenty people I made you call this morning and ask them to fax back by return in their own words what they thought of your approach and how they were influenced by it.'

John thought that he had given a bad impression to all twenty so was not particularly keen on this proposal, but he felt it would prove him right, so he agreed. The manager made the calls, in front of John, and later the faxes were brought to them by the secretary. Every reference was excellent, commending the caller on good manners, clarity of communication and professionalism. Feeling satisfied, the manager showed them to John, who read them in total disbelief. He put them down and said, 'I'll be damned, everybody does tell lies.'

The point of the story is that when you have a limiting belief, that belief will distort all new evidence, logic and argument until it fits with the belief. This is why belief is such an important area to peak performance. It can have this effect positively or negatively. Positively is when you belief so strongly in the inevitability of your success that no amount of evidence to the contrary or setback will affect your commitment.

Imagine that you had a belief so strong as to be a conviction that you could double your sales over the next six months. What do you think would happen?

C. The Effect Of Beliefs On Sales Professionals

All of my commercial experience supports the following belief: 'One person with the right beliefs will do far better than any of a thousand with better abilities and a keen interest, trying their best.' If you believe in your own success you will be empowered to achieve it.

If we make ten unsuccessful calls in a row, what will be the result of call eleven? If we make ten successful calls in a row, what will be the result of call eleven?

Now according to the 'numbers game' theory and mathematical logic, it should be like a roulette wheel. In other words, the outcome of each throw has no bearing on any other throw. In practice our previous experience sets us up with a belief that will strongly influence our subsequent performance.

Many of our beliefs are generalisations about our past, based on our interpretations of painful and pleasurable experiences. Often these beliefs are created by misinterpretation of past experiences. Once adopted these beliefs, however incorrectly founded, become a part of your inner reality and assume a direct influence on your behaviour.

Whenever something happens to you at work, your mind will automatically ask: 'Is this good or bad news for me? And what must I do to encourage good news and avoid bad news in the future?' You will then automatically form generalisations that determine your future behaviour. This is why so many sales people avoid cold calling. We make cold calls and experience failure and possibly unpleasantness from the recipient. This is bad news for us and we are then conditioned before the next call we make to expect failure and unpleasantness. How do you think we could break this cycle? Really think about this, as a solution that is produced by you will stand far more chance of success than my saying what works for me.

One person I know follows every call that goes well by writing the company name on a card in big letters, together with notes of what transpired, and sticking the card on the wall. The more calls he makes, the more cards go up on the wall. The more cards on the wall the more he is reminded of his successes and his positive progress through the day. That breaks the bad-news cycle for him – what did you come up with?

If you find yourself saying, 'I cannot....', ask yourself, 'What specifically stops me?'

Sometimes people are able to produce outstanding results in difficult circumstances simply because they don't know the task in question is considered to be difficult. I once employed a trainee called Richard and he asked me how many telephone canvass calls I expected him to make each day in addition to his other work. I jokingly said a 100, but he took me seriously. At the end of the month I looked at his records and he had in fact made a 100 calls per day average. I had not thought that possible previously, and had never attempted it personally, nor expected staff to achieve this level. Imagine how popular Richard was from then on amongst his colleagues!

Sales people may already have a lot of capabilities to influence their results, but if they don't *believe* they have those capabilities they will probably fail to use them.

Another point to consider is that the beliefs that others have about us will affect us. This has been tested by telling the managers of two different yet comparable sales teams that their team is well above and well below average respectively. That belief of the manager is transmitted. Have you ever had a teacher, manager, parent who believed that you would have difficulty at something? I have observed in a large sales team that the top performer starts attracting a certain awe and respect. The others start believing that his figures are the highest achievable and aim towards them without really expecting to reach them.. That is because 100% efficiency at anything is near impossible, (Or is that perhaps just my limiting belief). His figures certainly become their limiting belief.

People who have similar experiences may respond very differently. Many sales managers deal with the *symptoms* (average sales results, aversion to client visits, avoidance of cold calling). The *cause* in all of these cases could well be a limiting belief that is holding the representatives back. Alternatively it could simply be a lack of training and experience. Knowing which is the challenge that separates average managers from the superb.

Here are some limiting beliefs that I have personally changed for clients.

Symptom	Possible Limiting Belief
Average Sales Results.	I am an average sales person. I cannot do better because I don't have very good clients. I have always performed at this level so I always will.
Aversion To Client Visits.	I am not very good at meeting people. My gender is against me when I visit clients. I need all the information at hand to give a good account of myself. Clients on their home ground will be in a stronger position than me.
Avoidance Of Cold Calling.	I will be rejected on nearly every call. Cold calling is always boring. People hate being called by someone they don't know trying to sell them something. If they wanted our products, they would ring.

D. Beliefs Of Top Performers

The following questions are taken from a seminar I gave recently:

- 'Who here believes that they cannot consistently be the top sales-person in their company? Hands up.'

- 'Who here believes that they cannot double their last six months' sales in the next six months? Hands up.'

The majority put their hands up. I then explained: 'If you put your hand up all you have to do is replace those limiting beliefs with empowering ones, and your performance will significantly increase. Many salespeople are trapped by their own past; it sets the limits for them.' A key belief for top performers is:

The past does not equal the future.

What is the one belief you could change right now that would make the biggest difference in your career? Write it below:

....

....

Sales superstars are distinguished by their beliefs. Here are a few examples:

- Failure is feedback, which leads to learning and thus improvement.

  I know of a man who started a small business, worked all hours, despite advice from family and friends to get a regular job, and eventually, despite initial successes, went bankrupt. How did that affect him? What do you think his family and friends were telling him? What encouragement do you think he got from them to start another business? What financial support do you think he got from anyone? What do you think he did?

  He started another small business. What do you think happened to it? It went bust, that's what happened. Now, would you lend this guy money for a new venture? How do you think the banks reacted to him? Would you say that he was a gifted entrepreneur with a Midas touch?

  Shortly after his second bankruptcy he got into the motor trade in a small way. His name, Henry Ford! He used failure to learn; the more failure, the more learning. The more learning, the more success.

  If I look at my mistakes with reference to my objective and my other successes then they are valuable feedback. As such I can learn and improve my future performance. Eventually I am going to get all the results that I want, anything that gets in the way is feedback pointing me back on the right track.

- Setting clear objectives with an equally clear timetable is essential.
- Planning long-term produces better results long-term.
- In every adversity is a hidden opportunity.
- Losing a deal means you are a loser like eating carrots means you are a rabbit.

- I make it happen by taking action.

  Positive thinking alone is not enough; you need to take action. Things don't get better by themselves; they get better when some-body takes action. In a recession, or even during a boom in some instances, I have heard sales people say, 'I can't wait until things get better', or 'I hope my current problems go away or I'm not going to make any deals'. High achievers take the necessary appropriate actions to make them go away. Problems that go away by themselves have a habit of coming back by themselves. If the situation is not working for you almost anything else you do is more appropriate.

- Commitment is the key to excellence.
- Before my results change I have to change.
- Knowledge is only power when it is acted upon.
- Always give more than you expect to receive and you will receive more.
- I can go with flow of life or determine it.

  Successful people control their outstanding results, because they make their own luck. Then average performers accuse them of being lucky.

- Anything is possible.
- I alone am responsible for my results.
- Whatever someone else can achieve I am capable of doing much better.
- Limited beliefs create limited people.
- Your beliefs will expand or limit the beliefs of your client. If you believe that you are benefiting him, so will he.
- Belief in success is essential, techniques only help.

Adopt these beliefs; paste them on the wall; constantly be reminded of them. You will adopt the beliefs of top sales superstars.

E. Supporting And Limiting Beliefs

Empowering Beliefs

* I am capable of achieving everything that I want.
* I constantly seek to improve.
* Nobody has any advantages over me.
* I don't know it all. I can learn from everyone I meet.

An attitude of constant and never-ending improvement will produce excellence. Think of a time recently that you made a sales presentation and it did not go as well as you would have wished. What could you have done differently? What did you learn from the experience? If you were in that situation tomorrow, what would you do differently?

Limiting Beliefs

* I know it all.
* I am too old to learn new techniques.
* I can't....
* I don't....
* I'm no good at....

In my first position as a recruitment consultant I asked the company's top performer the following question. Annual figures were just out and he was personally responsible for £205,000 worth of invoices for permanent placements. 'What do you think is the highest possible placement figure you could achieve?' He responded, 'Well, looking at it logically, taking into account all the various factors, the highest possible is about £135,000.' He was then off talking to someone before I had a chance to ask him what he meant. Top achievers are not interested in what's 'possible' – they are interested in what they want to achieve. What is 'possible' is a limiting belief as far as they are concerned and they do not waste valuable time with it. After Henry Ford was declared bankrupt for the second time, did those around him consider it possible that he would build one of the world's biggest companies. Did British soldiers in the Falklands, ordered to sail 6,000 miles in a wild ocean and charge uphill into fortified positions outnumbered ten to one, stop to consider if it was possible? Of course not. What's 'possible' is an extremely limiting belief.

Empowering beliefs +
Knowing what to do +
Taking action   +
Feedback + Flexibility
_____

= Achievement of your goals

Think of something that you want to do but are holding back from because of past failure or concern. You are afraid that you might fail. If you knew that ultimately you would succeed, what would you not attempt?

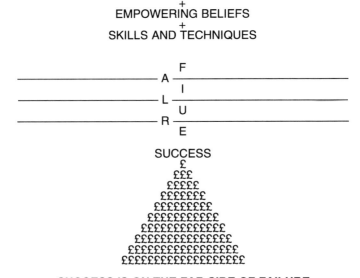

SUCCESS IS ON THE FAR SIDE OF FAILURE

F. How To Make Your Beliefs Supporting

Changing a limiting belief is like scoring a major deal. First you have to find a major customer – or in this case, find the limiting belief. In other words, establishing the limiting beliefs that are holding you back is easier said than done. This is because they can be buried deep in your subconscious and when they were being created you were not consciously aware of it.

Roger Bannister is famous for breaking the four-minute mile barrier. What is less known is that soon afterwards *hundreds* of people went on to achieve the same feat. Why do you think that was? When we believe something, by definition we stop questioning it. So how do you think we can start to change it? We question the validity of the belief. And if you question anything enough you will begin to doubt it, as contrary evidence mounts. What you are really doing is creating an alternative belief which has a cancelling-out affect.

Ask these questions both to yourself and to colleagues and friends:

- What advantages do others have?
- What is my weakest attribute?
- What stops me from being the company's top performer?
- What are the company's top performer's beliefs?
- What am I not the best at?

Amongst the answers to these questions you will find your limiting beliefs. It is usually easier to do this exercise in pairs; and remember that when we are talking about limiting and supporting beliefs, it is of no interest whether they are true or not. If you believe them they are true for you.

Most major improvements in sales performance, in my experience, begin with a change in beliefs. The easiest way to change a belief is to associate substantial 'bad news' with the old belief.

- Create doubt by questioning.
- Think of exceptions to the old belief.
- Apply Verbal Aikido to look at the belief from a different perspective.

What we want to do now is collect as much evidence as possible to contradict the limiting belief and to support a new empowering one. So make these challenges to your limiting beliefs:

- How is this belief ridiculous or absurd?
- Do the top sales people in my company hold this belief?
- What will it cost me to keep this belief?
- Can I think of any clear exceptions to the belief?
- What caused me to have this belief in the first place? Do the assumptions still hold?

Now we replace the old belief with a new empowering belief, by finding as many reasons with as much evidence as possible to support the new belief. To help create and develop your empowering beliefs, ask yourself:

- What evidence supports this belief?
- When have I known it to be true?
- Who do I know who has this belief?
- Why do they believe it?
- Do the top sales people I know hold this belief?
- What would happen if I firmly held this belief?

G. A Belief Change Exercise.

The following is the abridged transcript of a coaching exercise I performed recently for a client who wanted more empowering beliefs. It provides a good example of the way that you can go about changing your own beliefs. (See H. below, to apply the process to your own beliefs)

McMillan: List three beliefs you have, first limiting and second supporting your performance.

Client:

Limiting beliefs
1. £10,000 is the maximum sales I could possible achieve in a month.
2. I am below average at cold calling and hate it.
3. The competition have clear advantages over us.

Supporting beliefs
1. I can maintain enthusiasm and drive after a setback.
2. People like me.
3. I sincerely care about my customer's best interests.

McMillan: Now look at the three limiting beliefs listed, and list three beliefs that you would prefer to have.

Client:
1. Whatever result I can achieve I can do 10% better the following month.
2. I am exceptionally talented at cold calling and love it.
3. Whatever resources the competition has it is no match for my determination, dedication and enthusiasm.

McMillan: (referring to the first limiting belief, '£10,000 is the maximum sales I could possible do in a month.'): Tell me in your own words everything that is ridiculous or absurd about this belief?

Client: Uh, well, nothing – that's why I believe it.(Eyes move up and to the left, indicating that he is accessing visual memories.)

McMillan: If you could see something absurd about it, what would that be?

Client: Well, I suppose that so many things could change making it easier to achieve... and therefore it *is* ridiculous in a way.

McMillan: What kind of things?

Client: You know, inflation could make it easier.

McMillan: What else?

Client: Lots of things.

McMillan: Go on.

Client: A major competitor goes bust, if we had better marketing, a better corporate brochure would help. (Eyes now going to the right side indicating to me he was constructing ideas.)

McMillan: What else could change?

Client: If I changed my belief. Ha, Ha.

McMillan: So you are happy to accept that if you can change your belief, then you already have the requisite abilities to exceed £10,000 per month.

Client: I suppose so.

McMillan: What else could change?

Client: Well, if I had more confidence in my own abilities.

McMillan: How could your confidence be improved?

Client: Well, if I exceeded £10,000 per month it would automatically go up.

McMillan: OK. To get around that catch 22, let us pretend. I want you to close your eyes and imagine that last month you did £12,000 worth of sales. Imagine your boss is talking to you, what would he be saying? What would you be saying? What would it feel like?......

Now, bearing in mind that our brain's circuits are the same for imagining fiction as for imagining reality, using imagination in this way can be a very powerful tool. As long as I can the client to make the experience as vivid as possible the effect will be as though it were true. I continue to do this by talking him through all the internal sensory experience, i.e. using visual, auditory and feeling languages, and we return to the interview a little later...

McMillan: Now, how do you feel now about doing £12,000 next month? Do you think you can do it?

Client: Well, I'll give it my best shot.

McMillan: (Now, we are clearly not there yet, but we are in a better position than when we started.) What else can be done to increase your confidence?

Client: Praise. I'd like my boss and my peers to tell me how well I did sometimes – this may sound stupid but it builds me up.

McMillan: OK, so what could you do to get them to do that?

Client: I never thought that I could influence it. Ask them I suppose – after all, we have a team commission structure. But I think they will laugh.

McMillan: What else could change?

Client: I don't know.

McMillan: Who do you think might know?

Client: My wife always has good ideas with this sort of thing.

McMillan: OK. If she were here now sitting over there, what do you think she would say?

Client: That if I didn't keep avoiding cold calling with feeble excuses, I would have a bigger database to pitch to.

McMillan: OK. How exactly do you avoid cold calling?

Client: Well, I just avoid it.

McMillan: No, I mean exactly. If I had to step in for you tomorrow, how would I go about avoiding cold calling.

Client: Well, I imagine the people getting angry and not responding to what I say. (His face drops, his tone lowers and his voice slows to a drawl.)

McMillan: OK. What do you think you could do to change that?

Client: Go on a training course I suppose.

McMillan: OK, why don't you pursue that idea...Now, let us sum up where we have got to, so far. You think your limiting belief is absurd because:
  • Many things could change.
  • Inflation could erode the value.
  • A competitor could go bust.
  • You could gain more confidence.
  • You received training in cold calling.
That limiting belief is looking pretty silly isn't it?

Client: Yes, I see what you mean...

In the transcript above, I have only gone through the first challenging question, in order to demonstrate the idea. Clearly, by the time the other questions are exhausted the belief is all but gone. Note that if you are working in pairs it is important that the person being worked on comes up with their own solutions. Try not to make solutions and suggestions for them. The solutions have got to be produced and accepted by their unconscious mind in order for change to occur at a deep level. Now let us turn to helping the client create the first empowering belief that he would like to create: 'Whatever result I can achieve I can do 10% better the following month....'

McMillan: Do you know of anyone with that belief?

Client: Let me think.... Ah yes, Peter seems to take that attitude.

McMillan: OK. What did you think led him to that belief?

Client: Well, Peter thinks that there is no substitute for experience and that every day of every month there are lessons to be learnt. Therefore at the start of each following month he believes he is older and wiser and therefore works that little bit better. And in sales a marginal deal can mean a lot on the sales figures.

McMillan: What else do you think has led him to this belief?

Client: I don't really know, but the more I think about it the more I am convinced that he does have this belief that I would like. But I still believe that there is a limit to the number of calls you can make, the number of clients you can visit. etc., and at the end of the day everybody reaches their own plateau.

McMillan: Have you asked Peter himself about the belief?

Client: No, but I am certainly going to now that I have thought of it.

McMillan: What determines your plateau level?

Client: The sales target, I guess.

McMillan: And has there ever been a time when you exceeded it?

H. Your Turn To Change Your Beliefs

Write on the following pages your limiting and supporting beliefs and also the beliefs you would like to replace the limiting beliefs with. Then answer the following questions challenging each limiting belief and supporting the empowering belief that you want to change it with. I have also included questions on your present empowering beliefs, although these are not worked on specifically. Their purpose is to help establish your strengths, to help your thinking about beliefs process, to provide a basis for comparison between your current limiting and supporting beliefs, and to provide you with a final list of six empowering beliefs, which should be stuck up on the wall in your office for reinforcement.

Defining Current And Desired Beliefs

List 3 beliefs you have both supporting and limiting.

LIMITING BELIEFS
1..
2..
3..

SUPPORTING BELIEFS
1..
2..
3..

Now list 3 empowering beliefs you would like to acquire.

PREFERRED EMPOWERING BELIEFS
1..
2..
3..

Challenging A Limiting Belief

Ask the following questions:

- What examples can I think of when this belief was not true or did not apply?
  ....
  ....
  ....

- In what way is this belief ridiculous or absurd?
  ....
  ....
  ....

- Do the top sales people in my company hold this belief?
  ....
  ....
  ....

- What will it cost me to keep this belief?
  ....
  ....
  ....

- What exceptions are there to the belief?
  ....
  ....
  ....

- What caused me to have the belief in the first place? And do the assumptions still hold?
  ....
  ....
  ....

Creating And Developing The Empowering Belief

Ask the following questions of the belief you want to create:

- What evidence supports this belief?

  ....

  ....

  ....

- When have I known it to be true.

  ....

  ....

  ....

- Who do I know who has this belief?

  ....

  ....

  ....

- Do the top sales people I know hold this belief?

  ....

  ....

  ....

- What will happen when I hold this belief?

  ....

  ....

  ....

I. Group Belief Change

A company I visited recently with six sales staff had just spent the last two weeks agreeing targets with their Sales Director. The total target was £600,000, comprising individual targets between £60,000 and

£135,000. Initially the individuals had come up with their own figures totalling £420,000. The Sales Director got this figure up while maintaining agreement that they could do it. He knew that cooperation was essential for a target to be meaningful.

Having been invited to make a presentation, I asked about their new annual targets. I wrote the individual and total figures on a board. I then said, 'I want you to imagine that I have planted a miniature explosive device in your and your loved ones' heads. If these figures are not at least doubled by this time next year I will pull the switch and you and your loved ones will all die painfully. Believing this without any doubts, who thinks that they will do it?'

Six hands shot up.

I continued: 'What exactly can you do, that you are not doing now, that will enable you to accomplish this? What changes would have to be made? What changes would you risk trying?'

I then said, 'Imagine it is a year from now. I have returned and we are all drinking champagne celebrating this marvellous achievement. From this perspective looking back, What was it that you did that empowered you to produce these results?'

During the course of the afternoon the Sales Director could not believe the excited conversations, ideas and creativity that was coming forth from his staff. He was delighted with the result.

J. Final Note

If you are determined, the belief change system outlined in this chapter will work and will lead to significant improvements in your results. There are two more powerful NLP methods to produce a belief change: Timeline Reimprinting and Submodality Belief Change, which require the assistance of an experienced NLP Practitioner and are outside the scope of this book. If this is of interest to you, please write to the author at the address at the beginning of this book.

Bibliography

Awaken The Giant Within, Anthony Robbins, Simon and Schuster, 1992.

Beliefs, Robert Dilts, Tim Hallbom and Suzy Smith, Metamorphous Press, 1994.

Beyond Selling, Dan Bagley and Ed Reese, Meta Publications, 1987.

Change Your Mind - And Keep The Change, Steve and Connirae Andreas, Real People Press, 1987.

Changing Belief Systems With NLP, Robert Dilts, Meta Publications, 1990.

The Emprint Method, Leslie Cameron-Bandler, David Gordon and Michael Lebeau, Future Pace, 1985.

Frogs Into Princes, Richard Bandler and John Grinder, Real People Press, 1979.

Influencing With Integrity, Genie Z. Laborde, Syntony Publishing, 1987.

Introducing Neuro-Linguistic Programming, John Seymour and Joseph O'Connor, Harper Collins, 1993.

Magic In Action, Richard Bandler, Real People Press, 1984..

Modern Persuasion Strategies: The Hidden Advantage In Selling, DJ Moine and JH Herd, Metamorphous Press, 1980.

Patterns Of Hypnotic Techniques Of Milton H Erickson MD Vol 1, Richard Bandler and John Grinder, Meta Publications, 1977.

Patterns Of Hypnotic Techniques Of Milton H Erickson MD Vol 2, Richard Bandler, John Grinder and Judith DeLozier, Meta Publications, 1977.

Practical Magic, Stephen Lankton, Meta Publications, 1979.

Precision, Michael McMaster and John Grinder, Metamorphous Press, 1980.

Reframing, Richard Bandler and John Grinder, Real People Press, 1982.

Results On Target, Bruce Dilman, Outcome Publications, 1989.

Selling With NLP, Kerry Johnson, Nicholas Brierley Publishing, 1994.

The Structure Of Magic Vol 1, Richard Bandler and John Grinder, Science and Behaviour Books, 1975.

The Structure Of Magic Vol 2, Richard Bandler and John Grinder, Science and Behaviour Books, 1975.

Super Job Search (2nd edition), Peter K. Studner, Management Books 2000, 1996.

Time For A Change, Richard Bandler, Meta Publications, 1994.

Training With NLP, John Seymour and Joseph O'Connor, Harper Collins, 1994.

Unlimited Power, Anthony Robbins, Simon and Schuster, 1990.

Using Your Brain For A Change, Richard Bandler, Real People Press, 1981.

Index

CATCH THE SUCCESS EXPRESS

• Public Sales Training Courses
• Private Sales Training Courses
• Motivational Talks At Conferences/Meetings
• Consultancy
• Audio And Video Tapes
• Interactive CD-ROMs

For details of what Success Express currently offers please telephone or write to:

SUCCESS EXPRESS
35 Cook Road
Horsham
West Sussex
RH12 5GJ
Telephone: 01403 - 211866
Facsimile: 01403 - 257506
e-mail: training@succexpr.demon.co.uk